Charles Patteson's
Kentucky Cooking

Charles Patteson's
Kentucky Cooking

CHARLES PATTESON WITH
CRAIG EMERSON

Illustrations by Shirley Felts

HARPER & ROW, PUBLISHERS, New York
CAMBRIDGE, PHILADELPHIA, SAN FRANCISCO, WASHINGTON
LONDON, MEXICO CITY, SAO PAULO, SINGAPORE, SYDNEY

Library of Congress Cataloging-in-Publication Data
Patteson, Charles.
Charles Patteson's Kentucky cooking.
    Includes index.
1. Cookery, American—Southern style. 2. Cookery—
Kentucky. I. Emerson, Craig, 1928–   . II. Title.
III. Title: Kentucky cooking.
TX715.P3223 1988   641.59769   87-45761
                            ISBN 0-06-015830-1

FIRST EDITION

PRODUCED BY JANE ROSS ASSOCIATES, INC.
DESIGNED BY THE ANTLER & BALDWIN DESIGN GROUP

88 89 90 91 92   10 9 8 7 6 5 4 3 2 1

*To my aunts for their good nature and patience
and to Georgia Scott for her encouragement*

Contents

Introduction   12
The Derby   17
Traditional Specialties   43
Down-Home Cooking   65
The Hunt   93
The Harvest and Thanksgiving   113
Kentucky Inns   141
The Holidays   173
Appendix   219
Index   221

Acknowledgments

Writing a book like this is a journey through the memory (and, of course, through the recipe files). Not only does it bring to mind the flavors, aromas and scenes of long ago, it also brings into sharp focus the many friends—old and new—who have helped to shape and improve the book. First, there are the people who passed on their love of fine Kentucky food and their skill in the kitchen: Grandmothers Felts and Patteson; various aunts and cousins; our family cooks Georgia Scott, Vi Helen and Hazel Fisher, and Anna Smith.

Special thanks to Mimi Sheraton, who first suggested writing a Kentucky cookbook. Many people shared recipes and additional cooking expertise: Mildred Eblen Elliot, Helen Garvin Donnelly, Elizabeth Graves Sanders, Florence Felts, Mabel Newton Felts, Betty Jo Gaddie Beard, Sondra Penn Bertram, Luci Blodgett, Kaye Bowles, Mary Howard Dismukes, Ann Barret Donnelly, Marion Flexner, Camille Glenn, Marjorie Leichhardt, Mitchell Leichhardt, Winnie and Richard Allen Sanders, Elizabeth Eblen Sarfati, Emily Edwards Sergent, Martin Shallenberger, Mildred Wood Turner and Helen Witty.

There is a lot of work, plain and fancy, in creating a book like this one and the following people deserve acknowledgment.

Thanks to Sara Stamm, Basil Fattell, Maggie Lewis and George Mittendorf, who tested recipes and suggested changes where needed.

Liz Stone and Sheila Johnson of the Brooklyn Public Library were most helpful with the research, and John Dowling cast a critical but encouraging eye over the text.

There is nothing more reassuring to a cookbook author than to know that a food authority with the expertise of Mardee Regan has edited the manuscript; Frances McLaughlin helped fit the parts in their proper places; and without Jane Ross we never could have pulled this project together.

Many people contributed with lots of encouragement, not to mention research and/or manuscript typing: August Gold, Jane Heyman, Roberta Janes, Judi McMahon, Ellen Mait and Hydie Hately Prugh.

And thanks to the very long list of people who helped by tasting and commenting on these dishes. You are too numerous to mention, but you know who you are!

Charles Patteson's
Kentucky Cooking

*T*his book came about because my hobby is cooking. I'm a native Kentuckian—transplanted, unfortunately—and sometimes the best recipe for a case of homesickness is just any recipe with the flavor of Kentucky. I live in New York City now, and every cuisine in the world is available here. I've tried most of them. I've also sampled a good many during my travels here and there, and since I don't wish to sully Kentucky's reputation for honesty and fair-mindedness, I have to admit that there's some wonderful dining available at substantial distances from my old Kentucky home. But I've found that of all the varied foods I serve while entertaining in my New York home, the ones that disappear fastest are generally those from back home. And of all the many occasions on which I entertain, the buffet receptions I hold each year on Derby Day and New Year's Day—for which I serve only authentic Kentucky cooking—are by far the most enthusiastically attended. So I've reached the conclusion that the appeal of Kentucky cooking is practically universal.

The wonderful cuisine associated with Kentucky is the product of many influences. First among them is the strain of English and Scotch-Irish cooking of the pioneers who emigrated from the Eastern seaboard, bringing with them dishes served in New England, Pennsylvania and the tidewaters of Virginia, Maryland and the Carolinas. This basic cooking repertoire was substantially added to and modified by generations of black cooks, whose native dishes and seasonings helped produce a new and cosmopolitan food

Introduction

tradition. Some of the dishes using game, corn or native greens show evidence, too, of traditional American Indian cooking of the area.

Kentucky cooking is also very much influenced by the cuisine of France, dating back to Thomas Jefferson's ambassadorship and an 1825 visit to the state by the Marquis de Lafayette, whose hostesses sent away for French recipes to make him feel at home. Louis Philippe's prolonged stay in Bardstown before he ascended the French throne further reinforced the interest of Kentucky's socially prominent families in French cuisine. Throughout its history, the great rivers bordering Kentucky have served as mighty highways from the South, bringing Father Marquette, New Orleans cooking and jazz to Louisville. In fact, the royal house of France lent its name both to Louisville and to Kentucky's foremost liquor, bourbon whiskey, which is used extensively in the preparation of many of the state's most characteristic dishes.

So we boast a long line of cooks from various culinary traditions, making the best of Kentucky's marvelous foodstuffs—cornmeal, wild turkeys, branch lettuce, freshwater fish, raspberries, walnuts, snap beans, molasses and rich cream. From these materials, has evolved the distinctive cuisine identified with Kentucky; a style of cooking that not only keeps body and soul together but makes eager eaters bellow for more. (Diners of more refinement have been known to scrape their plates until the painted roses squeak.)

I learned to cook while still a child. Since my mother died when I was very young, I suppose you could say that I was taught to cook by proxy by my Grandmother Patteson. Though she had died before I was born, she had taught cooking to her own cook, Georgia Scott, and Georgia in turn taught me. In addition, I spent a lot of time in the kitchens of my Grandmother Felts and various loving aunts. In all of these households it was standard practice to make fresh, hot biscuits every morning for breakfast. Ordinarily there was a choice of desserts available from the pie safe, the cake stand and the cookie jar that never stood empty. Hams and country sausages hung in smokehouses and the cellars were lined with shelves of home-canned fruits and vegetables, jellies, pickles and preserves. So from my relatives and their cooks and from the extended family that constitutes small-town living, I picked up recipes (generally called "receipts" in my hometown) and cooking techniques from quite a number of women and one man, James Miller Williams. He was the grandson of slaves and he worked for my father and for his father before him. James wasn't a cook, but he always took great pride in personally preparing the more strenuous specialties—beaten biscuits and the best home-churned ice cream I've ever tasted.

In my mind's eye I can still see various combinations of these dear people moving about in their big old country kitchens with a sure, efficient grace, chatting and laughing together. From them I learned cooking as a set of skills and as a lifelong joy.

Most of the recipes in this book were accumulated over generations by members of my family. My ancestors didn't move to Kentucky: Kentucky came to them, since they were already living in the western part of Virginia when it was sectioned off to become the state of Kentucky in 1792. During all the time that my family has been living there they have been eating well, and various people have had the splendid good sense to write down and cherish the favorite recipes of generations of cooks.

Many of the recipes in this book have had to be reworked for use in the modern American kitchen. Not only family recipes, but even some found in old cookbooks have shown a happy-go-lucky disregard for exactness that just assumes that the reader is a born cook of long experience. "Add enough flour 'til it looks right" may have seemed a sufficient instruction to my great-grandmother, but is clearly lacking in modern terms. I've tried to arrive at what she intended by experimenting with the recipe, as I have with another from an old cookbook from a long-ago time that confidently ordered, "Stir in a nickel's worth of cinnamon."

That brings up another point about cooking Kentucky style: attitude. Kentucky is not only a state of the union but a state of mind. What you need to do is relax. Good Kentucky food, like good food anywhere, depends on using natural ingredients and knowing that Mother Nature doesn't operate with scientific exactness. If you were making an apple pie filling, you might want to combine apple slices, brown and white sugars, butter, cinnamon, nutmeg and perhaps other things. Exactly how much sugar to add, or how much of the spices, is impossible to say, since the sweetness or tartness of the apples has a lot to do with it. So just go at it with some dash and flair and remember that both very sweet apple pies and very tart apple pies have their enthusiasts.

Now when you get into the spirit of the thing, with the relaxed attitude of a Kentuckian and the devil-may-care outlook of a riverboat gambler, I hope you'll also bear in mind that for Kentucky hospitality a pleasing presentation of food is important. Kentucky food isn't fussy or pretentious and there isn't much call for spun-sugar swans, but when it's Derby Day in Louisville a visitor could go snow-blind from the shine on the mahogany, the polish on the silver and the gleam of the table linens. Even if your household arrangements don't run to heirloom furniture and sterling trays, a festoon of parsley or watercress dresses up a platter, and a bowl of fresh flowers is a fixture on Kentucky tables.

This book, then, will tell you about what we cook. There are extended notes on some of our favorite ingredients including bourbon whiskey and country hams. You'll find recipes for the special dishes Kentuckians serve on occasions like Thanksgiving and Christmas and above all, Derby Day. And you'll see where Kentuckians enjoy their sumptuous food—the handsome old homesteads and famous inns of Kentucky. We'll also explore some of the byways of our cooking tradition, such as soul food Kentucky-style and traditional hunt breakfasts.

By the time you've finished this book, you should know how to cook and dine like a true Kentuckian, whether you live in Bardstown or Bowling Green or on the peak in Hong Kong. And that's important because, as Georgia Scott once said to me, "Honey, if you're not in Kentucky, you're just hangin' over the edge."

CHARLES PATTESON

The Derby

Spring comes early in Kentucky, so that by the first Saturday in May, the date for the running of the Kentucky Derby, the season is well advanced and the whole state is at its best. Tulips and other early spring flowers are at their peak but the 80 degree temperatures bring out the roses, too. Flowering trees and shrubs—redbud, dogwood, quince and apple—are in blossom and azaleas and rhododendrons are everywhere. Lilacs fill the air with fragrance. The great stands of hardwood trees are in full leaf and the bluegrass, which gives the state its nickname, is lush and shining (and actually blue) in the warming glow of the May sun. It is the perfect time for a holiday and a chance to "kick it on out," and Kentuckians have been doing just that every year since 1875. There's a feeling of excitement for weeks in advance as people start sprucing up for the Derby. The world is coming to Louisville and Kentuckians believe in hospitality. Spring cleaning proceeds with a vengeance; windows are shined, silver is polished to a gleam, houses and fences are painted and everything takes on a festive air.

The Derby is the quintessential Kentucky celebration. I can't think of another event anywhere that focuses the attention of an entire state so completely or symbolizes it so universally, except perhaps a royal coronation, but the Derby takes place *every year*. The closest I can get to a comparison is to say that what Mardi Gras is to New Orleans, the Derby is to Louisville, though the "feel" of the two events is quite different. Derby week is tremendously exciting, but there's a fundamental sweetness about it and somehow it manages to be joyous and exhilarating without becoming frantic. Kentuckians just love their Derby and so does practically everyone else.

The Run for the Roses itself takes only a matter of minutes. After all, the whole point of a horse race is to demonstrate that these animals are *fast,* and every year the world's finest horses prove that by galloping the mile and a quarter at Churchill Downs in about two minutes. It's a gorgeous two minutes, but when you mention the Derby to me it brings more to mind than the thunder of hooves and the blur of racing silks hurtling toward the finish. The race is surrounded by days of excitement and fun, parties and music, drinks and hospitality and wonderful, unforgettable food.

The festivities start warming up on the Friday eight days before the race with the " 'They're Off' Luncheon" and the Derby Ball. From there on the week is filled with celebrations of all kinds. There's balloon racing, a rugby tournament, the Governor's Cup bicycle race, the opening of the Churchill Downs Spring Meet, picnics, a horse show, a mini-marathon, outdoor concerts with fireworks, dance cruises on the river, the running of the Kentucky Oaks ("the Kentucky Derby for fillies"), the annual steamboat race between the *Delta Queen* and the *Belle of Louisville,* the Pegasus Parade, the Derby trials and the Kentucky Colonels' Banquet. Of course there's a whole lot more going on, what with private parties and banquets, because the entire community is caught up in the spirit of the thing. And those are just the events *before* Derby Day. On the day of the race there's a gala breakfast, an afternoon of preliminary races at Churchill Downs, the Derby itself and any number of banquets and parties that night. On Sunday there is the Governor's Breakfast followed by the Kentucky Colonels' Barbecue, at which Kentucky's famed hunter's stew, burgoo, is always served. It is customary to dish up the burgoo in the guests' sterling silver julep cups when they empty them. At less elaborate affairs in suburban backyards the same thing is done but the cups may be tin cups with handles. Tastes just as good.

Most years I try to get back to Louisville for the Derby but it isn't always possible. When I can't make it, I always give a Derby Day party in New York. The race, which you can see more clearly on television than from the best box at the track, is the same race they see at Churchill Downs, and I make sure that the food on my table is the same food served at the best parties back home.

Derby week entertaining tends to be on a big scale. It's a chance to give everyone you know a wonderful time, and there is no point in cooking country ham and burgoo to serve just six. Get out your best linen, polish the silver, the dining table and anything else that isn't upholstered or ambulatory and set a buffet table. Roses and tulips are the traditional Derby flowers and they make a fine centerpiece. Now, what should you serve that is authentic and, even more important, delicious? The recipes in this chapter constitute the menu for a really magnificent traditional Derby Day buffet.

Start with the mandatory mint juleps, accompanied by some delicious little sandwiches and hot sausage balls. Burgoo, which is midway between a hearty soup and a stew, succeeds the juleps in the guests' cups as a first course. From there they can proceed to a sophisticated creamed chicken over waffles and to the superb country ham with bourbon glaze. Beaten biscuits are the traditional accompaniment, as well as Kentucky Sally Lunn bread, whose recipe dates back to colonial days. The ham is served at room temperature, and a cheddar-flavored grits soufflé supplies a hot dish for temperature contrast. There is a delicious selection of desserts on this buffet: Hickory Nut Whiskey Cake, Racing Silks Chocolate Pie, Pears in Red Wine, Lemon Squares, Apricot Sherbet and Marylou Whitney's Strawberry Fluff. Probably nobody will be able to try everything, but you can bet that nobody goes away hungry or thirsty on Derby Day.

MINT JULEPS

A mint julep is a fairly simple combination of bourbon whiskey, mint, sugar, water and ice, but as the architect Ludwig Mies van der Rohe said, "God is in the details," and it is the details of a julep that make it great. Be fussy. A julep really should be served in a frosted sterling silver julep cup. It holds 10 ounces and is usually slightly flared at the top. If you don't have silver cups (and most people don't) a heavy 10-ounce tumbler will do pretty well, although it won't be as thickly frosted. For a dozen juleps you will need:

12 julep cups or heavy 10-ounce glasses
Crushed ice
3 cups granulated sugar
1½ cups water
Handful of mint sprigs
24 ounces of 100-proof bourbon
12 sprigs of mint, for garnish

Place the cups or glasses in the freezer for several hours.

Fill the cups with crushed ice and return to the freezer overnight. Make a simple syrup by bringing the sugar and water to a boil. Reduce the heat and simmer for 5 to 10 minutes, until clear and thick. While still hot, stir in the handful of mint sprigs; allow to cool. Strain the syrup into a small pitcher; discard the mint.

Fifteen minutes before serving, remove the cups or glasses from the freezer. Pour 2 ounces of bourbon and 2 ounces of syrup into each ice-filled cup and decorate with a sprig of mint. Allow to sit for a few minutes until a good coat of frost forms on the outside and then serve.

NOTE: If you are using glasses, you can achieve a better frost if you wet them before placing them in the freezer the first time. Let freeze overnight. Fill with crushed ice the next day and return to the freezer for 30 minutes.

Makes 12 mint juleps

Savory Sandwich Spreads

The following sandwich fillings are excellent spread on beaten biscuits or melba toast rounds. They can also be made into small square, round or triangular sandwiches.

BENEDICTINE SANDWICH SPREAD

You may be expecting to find Benedictine liqueur in this recipe, but in fact it has no connection with the Benedictine order of monks. Created by Miss Jennie Benedict, a well-known Louisville caterer, this spread is traditionally dyed green with food coloring, but our family uses spinach leaves to get the desired effect. This recipe is easily made in a food processor.

1 medium cucumber, peeled, halved lengthwise and seeded
2 large packages (8 ounces each) cream cheese, at room
    temperature
½ small onion, grated
Dash of salt
Mayonnaise
Finely minced spinach or parsley leaves (optional)

Grate the cucumber and squeeze the pulp to remove the excess water. Combine the drained pulp with the cream cheese. Add the onion and the salt. Stir in just enough mayonnaise to make a smooth spread. Add enough minced spinach or parsley for an attractive green color.

Makes about 2 cups

PIMIENTO CHEESE SANDWICH SPREAD

10 ounces sharp cheddar cheese, grated
½ cup very finely chopped green olives
¼ cup minced pimientos
½ cup mayonnaise
Dash of Worcestershire sauce

In a food processor, meat grinder or by hand, combine all of the ingredients and mix well. Refrigerate until ready to use.

Variation: Add ½ cup finely chopped or ground pecans to the mixture.

Makes about 2½ cups

SAUSAGE BALLS

These are served hot with drinks. In my opinion, they are best when made with a spicy sausage in order to build a little internal fire for the frosty juleps to quench.

2 cups all-purpose flour
1 tablespoon plus 1 teaspoon baking powder
¼ cup vegetable shortening or lard
12 ounces hot sausage (see Note)
1 cup grated sharp cheddar cheese
⅔ cup milk

Preheat the oven to 350°. In a bowl, sift together the flour and baking powder. Cut in the shortening until the mixture resembles coarse crumbs. Add the sausage and cheddar cheese. Mix well. Pour in the milk all at once. Stir until the mixture begins to pull away from the sides of the bowl.

Turn the mixture onto a lightly floured board and knead for about 30 seconds. Form into bite-size balls. (Can be frozen at this point until ready to bake.) Place on a baking sheet. Bake for 12 to 15 minutes, until browned. Drain on paper towels.

Serve hot or at room temperature.

NOTE: This recipe is best made with homemade sausage. See sausage-making instructions (page 121) for this recipe. If you don't make your own, buy a good grade of hot bulk sausage or link sausage and remove the casings.

Makes about 3 dozen balls

TAYLOR COUNTY BURGOO

I've been eating burgoo all my life and no two burgoos are exactly alike. Indeed, no two burgoo *recipes* are exactly alike because this is a frontier dish, a hunter's stew made from what was available. It featured the game the land afforded, cooked with the vegetables in season. Squirrel, rabbit, turkey, possum, duck, venison and bear have gone into burgoos along with domesticated birds and animals. A great burgoo tends to be varied, nutritious, interesting and inscrutable. Some of the results of these impromptu combinations were so memorable that a tradition of parties featuring burgoo survived long after the campfires and the forests teeming with game became subjects of nostalgia.

In general, however, most burgoo recipes have some charac-
teristics in common. They are simmered slowly for long periods.
They almost always combine at least one kind of fowl with at least
one kind of red meat. They have a variety of vegetables, the most
commonly used being tomatoes, lima beans, onions, potatoes, okra
and corn. And they are usually highly seasoned with peppers, curry
powder, filé powder, bourbon, spices, herbs and/or prepared sauces
like Worcestershire or Tabasco. In other words, it's pretty much
dealer's choice for the cook, and if you have a guinea hen or a leg
of lamb or a possum or some turnips that you want to throw in,
feel free.

1 whole stewing chicken (4½ to 5 pounds)
4 cups beef stock or broth
6 large ripe tomatoes, cut up
2 medium onions, unpeeled
2 teaspoons curry powder
1 tablespoon freshly ground black pepper
1 tablespoon coarse (Kosher) salt
1½ cups bourbon
2 skinless boneless chicken breasts, cut into large pieces
1 cup diced country ham trimmings (optional)
2 cups fresh or frozen corn kernels, thawed if frozen
1 cup diced raw potato
2 cups shelled fresh lima beans
2½ cups okra, trimmed of stems and halved lengthwise
1 tablespoon filé powder (optional)

Place the chicken in a large stockpot with the beef stock and
enough water to cover. Bring to a boil over high heat. Reduce the
heat to a simmer and skim off the foam as it rises to the surface.
When the broth is clear, add the tomatoes, onions, curry powder,
pepper and salt. Cover partially and simmer gently for 2 hours.

Add 1 cup of the bourbon, partially cover and simmer for another 2 hours.

Turn off the heat. Remove the chicken. Trim off and discard
the skin and bones. Reserve the meat in large pieces. Strain the
soup into another container, pressing the onion and tomato pulp
through the sieve into the broth. Discard the solids. Chill until
the fat can be readily skimmed from the surface.

Rinse the stockpot and return the soup to it. Add the remaining
½ cup bourbon, the reserved chicken meat and the raw chicken
breast meat. Add the ham, corn, potato, lima beans and okra. Cover
partially and simmer for 30 minutes. Adjust the seasonings.

The filé powder is used to thicken as well as flavor the stew, so if your burgoo is as thick as you want it, omit this ingredient. Filé powder is a Choctaw Indian discovery made from sassafras leaves. If you don't care for sassafras flavor, you can thicken the burgoo by cooking it down, uncovered. If you do use filé, add it only after the pot is off the heat or the filé will become stringy. Thus, add filé only to the amount of burgoo you plan to serve at once. Reheated burgoo containing filé will be gummy.

Serves 16 to 18 as a first course

BLUEGRASS WAFFLES

Waffles always strike me as a modern invention like ice cream cones and chocolate chip cookies, but in fact they go back at least to colonial days when they were cooked in treasured waffle irons over open hearths.

This is a good recipe for plain waffles. The amount of sugar called for helps to crisp them but is not enough to push the finished product into the dessert category, so they are suitable for use with either a sweet topping like jam or sorghum and butter or with a savory one such as creamed chicken.

2 cups sifted all-purpose flour
1 tablespoon baking powder
1½ tablespoons sugar
¾ teaspoon salt
1½ cups milk
2 eggs, separated
¼ cup melted vegetable shortening

In a bowl, mix together the dry ingredients. Stir in the milk and egg yolks first, then the melted fat. Beat the egg whites until they form soft peaks. Fold into the batter with a rubber spatula. Cook in a preheated waffle iron.

Makes about 8 small waffles

CREAMED CHICKEN

Plain old creamed chicken is wholesome and nutritious, no doubt, and is one of those comforting foods when you're feeling sick or blue and would just like to return to childhood in flannel pajamas for a while. But if you're going to lay a festive table for company, plain old creamed chicken is a bit of a bore. I like to dress up P.O.C.C. with some added flavor, color and texture to bring it out of the nursery category and make it right at home in a silver chafing dish. I serve it over waffles.

¼ cup (½ stick) butter
1 cup chopped celery
1 cup sliced mushrooms
¼ cup all-purpose flour
2 cups half-and-half
1 jar (2 ounces) chopped pimiento
½ cup toasted slivered almonds
2 cups poached chicken breast, cut into 2-inch chunks
Salt and freshly ground pepper
2 hard-cooked eggs, cut up (optional)
¼ cup dry sherry

In a large skillet or saucepan, melt the butter. Add the celery and mushrooms and cook over low heat until just tender. Add the flour and stir until just slightly brown. Add the half-and-half and stir constantly until thickened, to make the cream sauce.

Add the remaining ingredients to the cream sauce and cook until heated through. Serve on waffles.

Serves 4

Country Ham

I found out some years ago that not everybody understands about country ham, probably the centerpiece of good dining in Kentucky. Once, when I wanted to express my gratitude to a family of New Englanders who had been especially nice to me, I sent them a fine, aged country ham from Kentucky. Time passed, but they never acknowledged the gift, which puzzled me. Eventually, I began to wonder whether there had been a mix-up in shipping so I asked whether the ham had arrived all right. My host, rather shamefaced, said that apparently something awful had gone wrong in transit and the ham had arrived covered with mold. They had given it a decent burial in the town dump and agreed to say no more about it to avoid embarrassing me. It was one of those "I didn't know whether to laugh or cry" situations, as those of you who know country hams will realize. For the rest of you who have not yet had the pleasure, the point is that aged country hams are *supposed* to be moldy, just as is Roquefort cheese. Most of the mold is on the rind, but the very best old hams have tiny white flecks in the meat itself, and that too is mold. Let me explain.

Before the development of refrigeration and freezing and freeze-drying and you-name-it that make up the modern techniques of food preservation, the only means of preserving meats for any length of time were salting, smoking, drying and pickling. Country ham uses the first three of these. By one of those fortuitous circumstances that crop up in food history, preserving meat from spoilage by these methods produced a food much more interesting than the fresh pork that our ancestors were trying to save.

The product usually thought of as ham by most Americans is the hind leg of a hog, pickled in a brine of salt, sugar, seasonings, various chemicals and sometimes a little artificial smoke flavoring. The meat is either soaked in this solution or the brine is injected into it with large hypodermic needles, or both. The resulting product has a rather sweet, mild, uninteresting flavor, a soft texture, a pink color and very little resistance to spoiling without refrigeration.

Country hams are different. Usually pigs destined to become country hams are fed on corn, but sometimes their diets include acorns, peanuts or even hickory nuts. The shape of the country ham also differs from ordinary hams since it includes part of the pelvis, which gives it its characteristic relatively long, tapering shape. Hogs are butchered at Thanksgiving time. The fresh hams are rubbed thoroughly with seasoned salt, a little sugar and finely ground black pepper and put in a cool, dry place to cure for 30 to 40 days. The salt slowly penetrates the meat and more salt is rubbed in at intervals. After the salt has had enough time to suffuse it, the meat is sometimes aged for a period of months before being smoked. The smoking process itself can take a month for the finest hams. Maple, hickory, apple wood and sometimes sassafras are used to produce the smoke that imparts an unforgettable flavor to the ham, darkens its color to mahogany, and further helps to preserve it. Mold begins to form on the surface of the rind. The Thanksgiving hams are considered usable by Derby Day, but the best hams are aged over the summer, when the "June sweats" occur and the meat grows drier and more flavorsome. The best hams are a year to 18 months old, although some are aged for up to two years, growing sharper and drier throughout.

We had our own smokehouse when I was growing up. It was out behind the house not far from the kitchen door and there were always lots of hams and sides of bacon hanging on hooks from the beams that crossed the ceiling. The smoking was done by building a fire in an old iron stove that vented into the room rather than up a chimney. James Miller Williams would get the fire going just right and then add damp hickory chips to the blaze, and we'd clear out and bar the door before the smoke got thick enough to smoke us, too. We would keep replenishing the fire and chips for about two weeks until James decided that we had smoked our hams enough. After the meats were smoked they remained hanging on their hooks to age.

My favorite dinner was ham and beaten biscuits and I always got to have that on my birthday (and fairly frequently on other, less exalted days as well). Georgia, my grandmother's cook, and I would go out to the smokehouse to choose just the right ham. She always took along a sharp old ice pick and she'd plunge it deep into each ham, withdraw it and sniff the point of the ice pick until she found one that met her standards. "Here, now," she'd say, "this one's been kissed by an angel." And she'd hand me the ice pick to smell. Sure enough, the birthday ham always smelled *wonderful*—nutty, sweet, smoky and mysterious. And it always wound up tasting wonderful, too.

By the time a ham has aged to the point of perfection that Georgia was after, it is rather dry and hard and both lighter and leaner than when the curing started because much of the moisture in the meat was surrendered during the smoking and aging. The meat is very salty, very smoky and rather like leather. Never mind. Enough of this lost moisture will be restored and enough of the salt and smoke will be removed during the soaking and boiling of the cooking process to produce a texture that is firm but toothsome and a flavor that is utterly distinctive, nutlike, smoky, as addictive as potato chips and not at all like the soft and flabby flesh of a canned or processed ham.

Sometimes as I am unwrapping a country ham that I've ordered from Kentucky, I think of that rustic smokehouse filled with dozens of hams approaching perfection. It was like having the wine cellar of a *grand cru* vintner where every day the dusty treasures get a little better. For a moment I may get a bit nostalgic for the bounteous riches of a whole smokehouse, but then I reflect that one ham at a time is enough for anyone, if it's a good one.

HOW TO PREPARE A COUNTRY HAM

Cooking a country ham involves removing some of the salt it acquired in curing and restoring some of the moisture lost through smoking and aging. Consequently, the ham is usually boiled rather than baked. After boiling, it is sometimes baked briefly in order to set a glaze on the outside.

10- to 16-pound aged country ham
½ cup cider vinegar
1 bottle of beer, or 1½ cups ginger ale (optional)
Whole cloves (optional)
About 1 cup brown sugar
¼ cup cornmeal
1 tablespoon dry mustard
1 tablespoon freshly ground black pepper
2 or 3 tablespoons bourbon, pineapple juice or apricot juice

Put the ham under cold running water and scrub with a stiff brush to remove any loose mold. Place the ham in a large container and add cold water to cover. Allow to soak for 24 hours. Drain off the water and scrub the ham again, then wipe with a cloth soaked in vinegar to remove any remaining mold.

Place the ham in a large kettle or deep roasting pan with enough water to cover it completely. Add the vinegar and beer to help neutralize the salt flavor. Bring to a boil, cover and simmer gently for 3 to 3½ hours. Keep the ham covered with liquid by adding boiling water as needed. The ham is done when the small crossbone in the shank can be pulled out easily.

Let the ham cool to room temperature in its cooking liquid. This will take several hours.

Preheat the oven to 400°. Remove the cooled ham from the liquid. Cut off all of the rind except for a small band around the shank end that will serve as a handle when carving. Trim off the fat, leaving only a ¼- to ½-inch-thick layer. You may score the fat in a diamond pattern and stud with cloves if you wish, although this is not traditional for country hams.

To glaze the ham: In a bowl, mix together the brown sugar, cornmeal, mustard and pepper. Moisten the mixture with the bourbon. Spread the mixture over the ham and bake for 20 minutes, or until the glaze is bubbly and nicely browned. Watch the ham carefully during glazing to make sure the glaze doesn't burn; pour a cup or two of water into the pan if necessary. Country ham is best served at room temperature, sliced very thin, with the grain.

JAMES'S OLD SOUTHERN BEATEN BISCUITS

Unless you are from the South, whatever ideas you may have about beaten biscuits are probably wrong. (Incidentally, in Louisville many people habitually refer to these biscuits in the singular, e.g. "We're having ham on beaten biscuit," as though there were only one biscuit in Jefferson County.) "Beaten" doesn't mean whipped together for lightness with an egg beater or whisk; it means placed on a flat surface and pounded with a blunt instrument—a rolling pin or a tire iron will do—for 20 minutes or so. (Granny used to beat 'em with a musket.) The resulting biscuits are not light and fluffy and melt-in-your-mouth; they are dry and crisp and crunchy and just about the best things ever invented for serving tiny sandwiches of sweet butter and country ham or as crisp bases for any canapé spread or pâté.

The problem with beaten biscuits has never been in the eating but in the beating, though they are well worth the labor they require even when made the traditional way. Flailing away at a batch of biscuit dough is good for the arm, the soul and the disposition and may be why old-time Kentucky cooks tended to be so sane and cheerful—they worked off their aggressions and resentments before breakfast every morning. If you are willing to forgo these psychological benefits, however, and if you own a food processor, you can now make beaten biscuits with little more time and effort than it takes to bake them. So here we go.

You will need either a device called a steel-roller biscuit brake, an electric food processor or a rolling pin—and a lot of spunk.

4 cups all-purpose flour
½ teaspoon salt

Pinch of baking soda
½ teaspoon sugar
¾ cup lard
½ cup cold milk
½ cup cold water

Traditional Method: In a bowl, sift together the dry ingredients. Cut in the lard. Mix in the milk and water to form a stiff dough. Place on a sturdy, flat surface and beat with a rolling pin or iron rod, using 300 to 500 licks, or until the dough is smooth and "pops" or blisters. If you have a biscuit brake, crank the dough through the rollers until it reaches the same consistency. Follow the directions below to form and bake the dough.

Food Processor Method: Place the dry ingredients in the container of a food processor fitted with the steel blade. Pulse a few times to blend. Add the lard and whirl a few seconds until the mixture is mealy. With the machine running, add the milk and water through the feed tube and process for about 2 minutes, until the dough is shiny, elastic and rather sticky, not unlike pulled taffy. Follow the directions below to form and bake the dough.

Forming and Baking the Dough: Preheat the oven to 350°. Heavily flour a rolling surface (it is easiest to do this with a flour sifter). Roll out the dough ½ inch thick. Cut out small round biscuits with a cookie cutter (or a whiskey jigger) and use a fork to prick each one with three rows of holes. Place the biscuits ½ inch apart on an ungreased cookie sheet. Bake for about 10 minutes, until risen. Increase the heat to 400° and bake for about 15 minutes more, until slightly brown. Split the biscuits at once.

Makes about 4 dozen

KENTUCKY SALLY LUNN

Sally Lunn is the traditional name of a delicious and unusual bread with a pale, creamy crumb and a dark brown crust. Baked in a tube pan, it makes a festive sight; and unlike most yeast breads, it does not need to be kneaded. This bread is said to be named after its inventor, a woman who had a bake shop in Bath, England, in the eighteenth century. My friend, Marion Flexner of Louisville, who kindly gave me permission to use this recipe, tells me that the Kentucky version is lighter and fluffier than the original bread because it uses beaten egg whites. Marion should know; she is the author of six cookbooks.

½ **cup half-and-half**
1 **package (¼ ounce) active dry yeast**
½ **cup (1 stick) butter**
¼ **cup sugar**
3 **eggs, separated**
2 **cups sifted all-purpose flour**
1 **teaspoon salt**

Scald the half-and-half. Skim. Cool until lukewarm (105° to 115°), then sprinkle on the yeast and stir to dissolve. In a mixing bowl, cream the butter and sugar. One at a time, add the egg yolks, beating well after each addition. Beat the egg whites until stiff but not dry. Sift together the flour and salt. Add the flour and the milk mixtures alternately to the creamed butter/sugar/egg mixture. Gently fold in the egg whites.

Cover the dough with a tea towel, set in a warm place and let it rise until doubled in size. Turn into a well-greased 10-inch tube pan and let rise again.

Bake in a preheated 375° oven for 25 to 30 minutes or until nicely browned on top.

Serves 12

GRITS SOUFFLÉ CASSEROLE

Hominy grits, the familiar Southern breakfast staple (as in grits 'n' eggs) is one of the legacies of our American Indian heritage. Basically, grits is ground-up dried corn with hulls and corn germ removed. Dried grits is a bit coarser than cornmeal. It has comparatively little flavor of its own when cooked and this neutrality of taste makes it a versatile base for other flavorings. For example, this grits soufflé casserole derives its color and zest from cheddar cheese and can be used as the starch in a meal in place of such a dish as potatoes au gratin. It is meant to be served hot but is just as delicious served warm. Unlike most soufflés, it will not collapse—even if it's not served direct from the oven. And this dish, which puffs up and browns on top like any soufflé, looks very festive on the table.

6 cups water
1½ cups hominy grits
½ cup (1 stick) butter
1 teaspoon salt
8 ounces sharp cheddar cheese, grated
1 teaspoon Tabasco sauce
4 eggs, separated

Preheat the oven to 350°. Butter a 2-quart baking dish or bowl. Combine the grits, butter and salt with the water in a saucepan. Cook, stirring constantly, 5 to 10 minutes until thick. Remove from the heat. Stir in the cheese and Tabasco. Beat the eggs yolks until light and lemon-colored; fold into the grits mixture. Beat the egg whites until they hold stiff peaks. Gently fold them into the grits. Scrape into the prepared dish.

Bake for 1 hour, until set and browned on top.

Serves 6

ASPARAGUS VINAIGRETTE

Asparagus is in season at Derby time and most people can't get enough of it. I like to simplify my Derby Day preparations by making a large amount of Sauce Vinaigrette and using it to marinate my asparagus and to dress my salad.

For a buffet, allow about ⅓ pound of asparagus per person.

Wash the asparagus and cut off the woody part of the stalk (usually the bottom inch or two). If the stalks are thick, use a vegetable peeler to remove the outer skin halfway up the stalk.

In a large skillet, bring enough salted water to cover the asparagus to a boil. Add the asparagus and cook for 10 minutes or more, until the tips are just tender. You want the stalks to be a little crunchy. Drain immediately and rinse in cold water to stop the cooking. Let cool to room temperature.

Make the Sauce Vinaigrette (recipe follows). You will need about ½ cup per pound of asparagus. For a large buffet, multiply the recipe and make it with an electric mixer, blender or food processor. Marinate the asparagus in the sauce for 2 hours, turning occasionally. Serve on lettuce with a bowl of mayonnaise on the side.

SAUCE VINAIGRETTE

This is pretty much the standard vinaigrette recipe. You may be familiar with it, but here it is anyway, just in case you're not.

**2 tablespoons good white wine vinegar or a mixture of vinegar
    and lemon juice
⅛ teaspoon salt
¼ teaspoon dry mustard (optional)
1 to 2 tablespoons minced fresh green herbs, such as parsley,
    chives, tarragon or basil, or 1 to 2 teaspoons of the same
    dried green herbs, crushed or rubbed to a powder (optional)
6 tablespoons vegetable oil or olive oil
Big pinch of freshly ground pepper**

In a bowl, beat the vinegar with the salt, mustard and crushed dried herbs until the salt dissolves. Beat in the oil by droplets until emulsified. Season with pepper. If you are using fresh herbs stir them in and correct the seasoning just before dressing the salad.

(An alternative method is to place all of the ingredients in a screw-top jar and shake vigorously to blend thoroughly.)

Makes about ½ cup

Bourbon Whiskey

This chapter about the Kentucky Derby is probably a good place to tell you a little about what is probably Kentucky's best-known product—bourbon whiskey. (Please notice that "whiskey" is spelled with an "e"; Scotch whisky gets along without one.) We use bourbon a lot, much of it of course in drinks, of which the most famous is probably the mint julep. However, bourbon also appears as a flavoring in our cooking, as you can hardly help but notice throughout this book. You'll find it in recipes for candy (bourbon balls), for desserts (bourbon

THE DERBY **35**

cake), for condiments (bourbon jelly); even main-course dishes such as burgoo may be enhanced with bourbon.

When you cook anything containing spirits at 170° (a low simmer) or higher, it will lose its alcoholic content. So unless the bourbon is added as a last-minute enrichment it isn't likely to make Aunt Maude tiddly, though the whiskey does impart a special bouquet and a rich flavor. It isn't always easy to identify, but it can make the difference between a striking dish and a rather ho-hum one.

Bourbon, with its smooth and mellow subtleties, is the sophisticated offspring of very rough and uncouth antecedents. It was developed from a famous and hearty beverage still being made in the Appalachians and elsewhere, and known by various affectionate names, including white lightning, moonshine, corn squeezin's, corn likker and that good ol' mountain dew.

If you want to know what this colorfully named liquor is like, Irvin S. Cobb, a Kentucky humorist of a couple of generations back, said, "It smells like gangrene starting in a mildewed silo, it tastes like the wrath to come, and when you absorb a deep swig of it you have all the sensations of having swallowed a lighted kerosene lamp. A sudden, violent jolt of it has been known to stop the victim's watch, snap his suspenders, and crack his glass eye right across." Nevertheless, this raw distilled product was the comfort (and probably the curse) of our rugged ancestors on the frontier, although it was considered beneath the tastes of gentlefolk in the cities, who warmed their insides with wines, brandies, fortified wines such as sherry or port and, when they wanted a real jolt to forget the French and Indian Wars, high-proof rum.

Then, in 1789, a man of God and benefactor of the human race named the Reverend Elijah Craig decided he could produce a product just as intoxicating as corn likker but somewhat more refined, and he developed a new whiskey recipe. This historic event took place in Georgetown, in what was then Bourbon County, Kentucky Territory, State of Virginia. The kindly cleric's benefaction was made by combining ground corn and rye meal with boiling water, stirring mightily, cooling overnight and adding malted corn and barley. The malt acted on the starch from the ground meal to produce a sugar. Yeast was added and it fermented. When the fermented liquid was cooked in a still, the alcohol and the liquor boiled off, were caught and condensed in a coil, then put into containers and sold.

If you were to be served a glass of the Reverend Craig's product today you would probably call the Consumer Products Safety Board, since it would taste about like gasoline. But at the time, it was considered so superior to what people had been drinking, that Bourbon County whiskey soon developed a reputation for smoothness. Everything, as Einstein so cogently observed, is relative. Reverend Craig's cunning concoction had another thing going for it besides the rather crude recipe—the best water known for distilling whiskey. The quality of the water is of paramount importance in making fine whiskey, and the water in Kentucky is filtered by nature through many layers of limestone rock, making it just about perfect. Thus, all that the original bourbon formula needed was further refinement. Various small-scale distillers began tinkering with the recipe, each using his own proportions of grains, but always using corn as the principal one. A second distillation became common, making the whiskey smoother and more powerful.

At this point in its history bourbon was still a clear, colorless liquid and a pretty fiery one at that. Then some unsung hero, to whom I'm sure Kentucky would erect a monument if he or she could be identified, discovered that storing the whiskey in charred oak barrels gave it a warm, amber color, a smooth mellow quality and a distinctive flavor.

Soon distillers were vying with each other to take advantage of the increased popularity of bourbon whiskey by improving the product and putting their own brand name on it. While corn likker continued to be sold anonymously in earthenware jugs and glass Mason jars, bourbon whiskey appeared in glass bottles with the maker's name proudly displayed. Some of these original distilleries are still at the still, so to speak, and their brands have become world-famous. So coveted did bourbon become that Congress enacted a Federal law making it illegal to label any whiskey made outside Kentucky as bourbon. Thus, when the first Kentucky Derby was run well over 100 years ago, there was a well-established native libation available for toasting the winner, and the Derby and bourbon are still inextricably linked.

As to what bourbon is like, in case you'd rather do your research in the library than the bar, Bernard De Voto said of fine bourbons that "they wake delight like any great wine with a rich and magical plenitude of overtones and rhymes amid resolved dissonances and a contrapuntal succession of fleeting aftertastes. They dignify man as possessing a palate that responds to them and ennoble his soul as shimmering with the response."

HICKORY NUT WHISKEY CAKE

Two genuine treasures that are greatly appreciated in Kentucky cooking are hickory nuts and, as I've just told you at great length, bourbon whiskey. They are combined to advantage in this moist, flavorful cake. Bourbon is still plentiful, but hickory nuts are becoming a delicacy even in Kentucky. They're well worth today's high cost, however, for the sake of this traditional cake.

2 cups all-purpose flour
1 teaspoon baking soda
1 teaspoon ground cinnamon
2 teaspoons freshly grated nutmeg
½ cup (1 stick) unsalted butter, at room temperature
½ cup granulated sugar
½ cup packed brown sugar
6 eggs, separated
1 teaspoon fresh lemon juice
1 cup dried currants
1 cup golden raisins
2 cups coarsely chopped hickory nuts (use hazelnuts if you don't
   have hickory nuts)
½ cup bourbon whiskey
½ teaspoon salt

Preheat the oven to 300°. Butter 2 standard loaf pans. On a sheet of waxed paper, sift together the flour, baking soda, cinnamon and nutmeg; set aside. Cream the butter until soft and then cream in the sugars, a little at a time, until smooth. Beat the egg yolks;

add to the butter mixture. Stir in the lemon juice.

Mix the currants, raisins and nuts with the dry ingredients. Add to the batter, alternating with the whiskey. Beat the egg whites with the salt until they form soft peaks. Gently but thoroughly fold into the batter.

Divide the batter between the prepared loaf pans. Bake for 2 hours, or until the cakes pull away from the sides of the pans.

Makes 2 loaves; serves 20

RACING SILKS CHOCOLATE PIE

This pie is representative of a number of variations on chocolate-nut pies that are traditionally served at Derby time under various names, including Governor Collins's Pegasus Pie (page 171). Racing Silks Pie is especially smooth and rich and is unusual in that the pie shell is made of meringue.

PIE SHELL:

2 egg whites
⅛ teaspoon salt
½ teaspoon cream of tartar
½ cup sifted sugar
½ cup finely chopped pecans
½ teaspoon vanilla extract

FILLING:

½ cup (1 stick) butter, at room temperature
1 cup sugar
2 squares unsweetened chocolate, melted
2 whole eggs
3 egg yolks
1 teaspoon vanilla extract
Whipped cream and shaved chocolate for serving

Make the pie shell: Preheat the oven to 300° and lightly butter a 9-inch pie pan. In a bowl, beat the egg whites, salt and cream of tartar until stiff. Gradually add the sifted sugar and continue beating until stiff peaks form. Fold in the nuts and vanilla. Spread evenly in the pie pan, smoothing it up the sides of the pan a bit. Bake for 50 to 55 minutes. Cool on a rack.

Make the filling: Cream the butter and sugar in the top of a double boiler. Blend in the chocolate and set over simmering water. Add 1 whole egg and 1 egg yolk at a time, beating for 5 minutes after each addition. Add the final egg yolk and beat for 5 minutes. Remove from heat and add the vanilla. Pour into the cooled pie shell. Refrigerate overnight until set.

Serve with the whipped cream and chocolate shavings.

Serves 8

PEARS IN RED WINE

A friend of mine sampled these poached pears and said in a tone of wonder that the pears spoke to her. I've never figured out exactly what she meant, but my advice is that if your guests start hearing from the pears, you probably waited too long before filling the julep cups with burgoo.

10 ripe but firm pears (see Note)
3 cups dry red wine (cabernet or pinot noir)
6 tablespoons sugar
Dash of ground cinnamon
Lightly whipped heavy cream, for serving

Peel the pears and core them from the bottom, leaving the stems intact. Stand the pears in a deep heavy casserole or non-reactive saucepan large enough to hold them upright. Pour in the wine and add enough water to cover the pears. Add the sugar and cinnamon to the liquid.

Poach, uncovered, at the lowest simmer with the liquid barely moving, for 20 to 30 minutes, or until the pears are tender. Remove the pears to a serving dish. Boil the liquid down until it is thick enough to coat a spoon. Pour over the pears and allow to cool to room temperature. Serve with heavy cream, lightly whipped, on the side.

NOTE: The pears must cook in an upright position; they should not float on their sides. Ten happens to be the number of pears that fit nicely into the casserole I use. If your casserole is too large, surround the pears with a collar of folded aluminum foil.

Serves 10

APRICOT SHERBET

Although it is not necessary to form this in a fancy mold, it does make a more lavish presentation that way.

4 cups sugar
2 cups apricot nectar
2 cans (16 to 17 ounces each) whole apricots
24 juice oranges
6 lemons

Combine the sugar and nectar in a heavy saucepan. Drain the apricots, reserving the syrup. Pit the apricots if necessary. Add the apricots to the sugar and water and simmer gently to make a syrup. Let cool completely.

Squeeze the oranges and lemons and strain the juice. Remove the apricots from the saucepan with a slotted spoon. Purée them and return to the syrup. Add the orange and lemon juices and the reserved apricot syrup. Freeze in a manual or electric ice cream freezer according to the manufacturer's directions.

Serves about 24

STRAWBERRY FLUFF

A wonderfully elegant large scalloped meringue shell heaped high with a mixture of perfect strawberries and whipped cream, lavishly garnished with more berries and complemented with sherry custard sauce: This dessert, called "Strawberry Fluff," is always served at Marylou (Mrs. Cornelius Vanderbilt) Whitney's annual Derby Eve Dinner in Lexington, Kentucky. She was kind enough to permit me to pass it on to you.

MERINGUE SHELL:

6 egg whites, at room temperature
2 teaspoons vanilla extract
½ teaspoon cream of tartar
2 cups sugar

Preheat the oven to 225°. Combine the egg whites, vanilla and cream of tartar; beat until frothy. Gradually add the sugar, 1 tablespoon at a time, beating until stiff peaks form. Drop the meringue by ⅓ cupfuls, touching each other, in a ring around the edge of a 10-inch pie plate. Bake for 1 hour. Turn off the oven; cool in the oven for 1 hour. Carefully remove the meringue ring to a serving dish.

STRAWBERRY FILLING:

**2 cups heavy cream
1 quart fresh strawberries, hulled and sliced
1 quart fresh strawberries, hulled and left whole**

Beat the cream until soft peaks form. Fold in the quart of sliced strawberries. Spoon the mixture into the center of the meringue and arrange the quart of whole strawberries around the outside of the meringue. Serve with the chilled Sherry Custard Sauce (recipe follows).

SHERRY CUSTARD SAUCE:

**2 cups milk
6 egg yolks
¼ cup sugar
⅛ teaspoon salt
1 cup heavy cream
3 tablespoons sweet sherry
½ teaspoon vanilla extract**

Scald the milk in a double boiler over barely simmering water. Beat together the egg yolks, sugar and salt. Gradually pour the mixture into the milk and stir constantly over the hot water until thickened enough to coat the back of a spoon. Whip the cream until soft peaks form. Fold into the custard sauce. Stir in the sherry and vanilla. Chill.

Serves 10 to 12

Traditional Specialties

*I*n the corner of my grandmother's kitchen stood a big wooden flour barrel. When I was little, I used to stand on tiptoe and peer into the barrel to make sure the flour level wasn't getting low because I didn't want the endless stream of cakes, pies, biscuits and breads that flowed from that magic barrel to cease. A big tin flour scoop and a sifter were kept right in the barrel along with the flour. There was no thought of washing them up and putting them away after use because they never stopped being used. Flour for cakes was sifted directly into the scoop and went from there into a measuring cup; flour for pie crusts was never measured at all. My grandmother or anyone who cooked for her simply scooped what looked like enough flour onto a wooden table, added what looked like enough shortening and worked it in with the fingertips until it looked and felt right. She would sprinkle in ice water and mix the dough until it satisfied her, form a flat cake of it and be ready to roll it out after a short chill in the icebox. Amazingly enough, the system always produced exactly enough pastry for the number of pies needed, with just enough left over to make a little sugar tart for me. That's how I learned to make pie dough—by feel—and recipes for measuring it out strike me as artificial to this day.

I have read that there is a trend in American family life for each person in a household to eat separately, grabbing a snack on the way through the kitchen to someplace else. In small towns in Kentucky when I was growing up, it didn't work that way. Meals were served at mealtimes, mealtimes were ordained by Heaven, and everybody sat down to dine together.

In summertime the big meal of the day, called dinner, was served at noon. Dinner was a substantial meal, and when the noon chimes from the Methodist church rang out, fathers came home from town and everyone sat down at the table together. This was true everywhere: at our house and my grandmother's and all my aunts and uncles and all our friends and neighbors. It was true out in the country when I stayed with the Porters, who were the family that farmed some of my father's land as tenants and who rang a dinner bell at noon, not having the advantage of the Methodist's chimes. I was sure that it must be true even in China, where Chinese children sat down at noon to their exotic meals of egg foo yung, chop suey and fortune cookies. We were more likely to have something familiar, like Sausage-and-Cornbread Pie or fried chicken with corn pudding and baked tomatoes. This would be followed by dessert—Rhubarb Pie, or perhaps Buttermilk Cake.

Breakfast was also a hearty meal, featuring bacon or ham and eggs, usually with grits and a hot bread with butter and preserves. My Grandmother Felts baked hot breads twice a day, and three hundred sixty-five days of the year my Aunt Annie Garvin, who lived in a lovely old antiques-filled farmhouse, made fresh cream of tartar biscuits for breakfast. These are still my favorite of all the biscuits I know. They are just as fine cold as they are hot. I always make a bigger batch than I need for a given meal so I can enjoy some later.

Because the big meal was served at noon, the evening meal in summer, called supper, consisted of lighter foods and smaller portions. We ate at 6:00 P.M., long before the summer sunset. Some-

45

times on those warm evenings we had leftovers such as cold fried chicken. Sometimes we had cooling, light summery foods like Seafood Aspic served with a substantial, tangy hot vegetable such as Green Pepper Puddin'. Desserts would likely be the same ones served at noon.

We often had a variety of pies available. They were kept in a metal pie safe with perforated sides where pies could be cooled and stored safe from flies and with enough air circulation to keep them in good condition. I recently read that pies should be served as soon as possible after baking, and I agree they are at their prime that way, but don't overlook the pleasure of a wedge of yesterday's peach pie with thick country cream served for breakfast. That's a way to start the summer morning!

In winter, the pattern changed and we ate our big meal of the day in the evening, often substantial stick-to-the-ribs dishes such as Stuffed Cabbage or Pork Campbellsville-Style. I imagine the custom of big meals at noon in the summer originated on the farms to give the workers a chance to rest and rebuild their strength before returning to the fields, and in winter there was no need for such an arrangement.

Winter and summer we ate foods like the ones in this chapter and, indeed, like others throughout this book, most of which are traditional specialties in Kentucky and used in everyday dining. I've also included some Kentucky specialties for the ceremonial side of life: a simple wedding cake for the happy times, and a funeral cake for the sad ones.

You needn't adhere to these traditional recipes any more rigidly than you wish (see my Aunt Lizzie's riff on Salade Niçoise) except, perhaps, in the case of cakes. I remember one country woman of the old school whom I met in Kentucky. She was a traditionalist, even having named her three daughters Shirley, Goodness and Mercy after the Twenty-third Psalm. As near as I can figure, it was an attempt to ward off a lonely old age. She was famous for her beef stew, which she made with tomato juice. I mentioned that I usually used a dry red wine, instead. "Yep," she said, "you could do that." But as she turned away I heard her mutter under her breath, "Wouldn't be any good, though." So much for French cooking.

Summer Aspics

Shimmering, colorful and cool, clear aspics are wonderful for hot weather menus, and extremely versatile. When the weather is torrid, they are refreshing just to look at and, as a first course, they rejuvenate the heat-robbed appetite. By adding morsels of cooked chicken to chicken aspic or cooked, chilled shrimp, crab or lobster to seafood aspic before molding you can produce a light main course for a summer luncheon.

Aspics can enhance a platter of food in an easy but sumptuous way. Simply pour a thin layer of aspic in a pan and allow to set. Then cut the aspic into diamond shapes and use as a shimmering bed on which to place the main course.

If you don't want a clear jelly, substitute mayonnaise or sour cream for part of the liquid.

SEAFOOD ASPIC

1 envelope unflavored gelatin
1 bottle (8 ounces) clam juice
1 teaspoon fresh lemon juice
2 teaspoons dry sherry
¼ teaspoon salt
Dash of Tabasco sauce

Soften the gelatin in half of the clam juice. Bring the remaining ingredients to a boil in a nonreactive saucepan. Add the dissolved gelatin mixture to the hot liquid and stir to mix well. Mold and chill until set. Serve on a bed of lettuce with mayonnaise or use for garnishing the main dish.

Makes about 1 cup

CHICKEN ASPIC

1 envelope unflavored gelatin
1 cup fat-free chicken stock
½ teaspoon white wine vinegar
2 teaspoons Madeira or sweet sherry
½ teaspoon *glace de viande* (see Note)
½ teaspoon fresh lemon juice
¼ teaspoon salt

Soften the gelatin in half of the chicken stock. Bring the remaining ingredients to a boil in a nonreactive saucepan. Add the dissolved gelatin mixture to the hot liquid and mix well. Mold and chill until set.

NOTE: Frozen *glace de viande* can be purchased at many specialty food stores.

Makes about 1 cup

VEGETABLE ASPIC

2 envelopes unflavored gelatin
2 cups V-8 juice or tomato juice
1 teaspoon Worcestershire sauce
1 teaspoon white wine vinegar
3 to 4 tablespoons minced green bell pepper
3 to 4 tablespoons minced celery
3 to 4 tablespoons minced carrot

Soften the gelatin in half of the V-8 juice. Bring the remaining V-8, the Worcestershire sauce and vinegar to a boil in a nonreactive saucepan. Add the dissolved gelatin mixture to the hot liquid. Stir in the chopped vegetables. Mold and chill until set.

Makes about 2 cups

SAUSAGE AND CORN BREAD PIE

This is a hearty, informal one-dish meal prepared and served in a heavy cast-iron skillet. The corn bread expands to form a golden topping around the edge of the country sausage and vegetable filling.

SAUSAGE FILLING:

1 pound bulk sausage
¼ cup minced onion
3 tablespoons all-purpose flour
½ teaspoon salt
½ teaspoon pepper
½ cup corn kernels
½ cup minced green bell peppers
1½ cups tomato juice

Brown the sausage and onion in a heavy cast-iron skillet. Drain off the fat. Remove from the heat and stir in the flour, salt and pepper, blending well. Add the corn and peppers. Return to moderate heat and gradually add the tomato juice, stirring until thickened.

CORN BREAD TOPPING:

1 cup sifted all-purpose flour
½ cup yellow cornmeal
2 teaspoons baking powder
1 teaspoon salt
¼ cup shortening
1 egg
¾ cup milk

Preheat the oven to 425°. In a mixing bowl, combine the dry ingredients. Cut in the shortening, mixing thoroughly. Add the egg and milk and stir just enough to form a lumpy batter.

Bring the sausage filling to a boil in a heavy cast-iron skillet. Drop the corn mixture by spoonfuls around the edge. Bake for 20 minutes, or until the corn bread is puffed and very lightly browned.

Serves 8

COUNTRY DOVES

Doves are small, succulent birds that require careful cooking to avoid drying out. You'll need at least two per serving. This recipe is practically a one-dish meal. You could serve it with just a salad and bread and have the kind of supper my family enjoyed every autumn.

1 cup all-purpose flour
1 teaspoon ground marjoram
1 teaspoon salt
1 teaspoon freshly ground pepper
8 to 10 doves or squab, split lengthwise
½ cup (1 stick) butter
1 garlic clove, split
2 small onions, diced
1 cup chopped canned tomatoes
2 cups cooked white rice
4 cups chicken stock
½ teaspoon dried basil

Combine the flour, marjoram, salt and pepper in a large brown paper bag. Add the doves and shake until well dusted.

Melt the butter in a large skillet over moderate heat. Add the garlic and brown it well; discard the garlic.

Brown the birds quickly in the butter; set aside. Add the onions and brown. Add the tomatoes and stir for 2 minutes. Add the rice and stir until the rice is lightly browned.

Combine the chicken stock and basil. Place the doves in a large casserole. Stir in the rice mixture and chicken stock. Bring to a boil, stirring constantly. Reduce the heat to a simmer, cover and cook, without stirring, for 25 minutes. Arrange the mixture in a large deep platter and serve.

Serves 4 to 6

STUFFED CABBAGE

This is hearty and delicious fare for winter nights. Like most cabbage dishes I associate it with *Mittel Europa* or even Eastern Europe. I'm not sure how this recipe found its way to *Mittel Kentucky* and our dinner table, but I have a hunch it was part of the culinary heritage of my mother's side of the family. They, as I was frequently reminded whenever I told a lie, were descended from George Washington, but nevertheless included my Pennsylvania Dutch (which is to say German) great-grandparents who enriched the family menu with such foods as this.

1 head green cabbage
8 ounces ground sirloin
12 ounces ground pork
3 eggs, beaten
1 medium onion, chopped
½ cup cooked white rice
2 teaspoons salt
¼ teaspoon freshly ground pepper
About ⅓ cup milk
1 cup tomato juice
1 cup beef stock
¼ cup cider vinegar
1 bay leaf

Core the cabbage. Place in a deep pot and add boiling water to cover. Simmer for about 10 minutes. Drain the cabbage carefully. Pull off 16 to 18 of the largest outer leaves. Trim down the thick center ribs.

In a bowl, combine the sirloin, pork, eggs, onion, rice, salt, pepper and just enough of the milk to make a loose mixture. Put ¼ cup of the filling in the center of each cabbage leaf, roll up and tuck in the ends, making a neat package.

Preheat the oven to 350°. Place the cabbage rolls side by side in a shallow, well-greased baking dish. Combine the tomato juice, stock, vinegar and bay leaf and pour over the cabbage rolls. Cover and bake for 1 hour, until cooked through.

Serves 6

PORK, CAMPBELLSVILLE-STYLE

Pork, Campbellsville-Style, is the name I have given to a favorite dish of my Uncle Oma Goode (pronounced to rhyme with food). My Aunt Lena, his wife, was generally acknowledged to be one of the best cooks in Campbellsville and consequently had to entertain a lot to keep the title. When Aunt Lena and Uncle Oma were giving dinner parties or luncheons, they never served food as down-to-earth as this, but on an ordinary Tuesday night at home in February, my aunt was likely to prepare what my uncle liked.

This flavorful braised dish, like the German favorite sauerbraten, is marinated for a long time to infuse the meat thoroughly with its marinade. Unlike sauerbraten, however, the marinade is not sweetened and the meat employed is pork, not beef.

3 cups dry red wine
1 cup red wine vinegar
3 carrots, sliced
2 large onions, sliced
4 garlic cloves, crushed
6 bay leaves
1 bunch of parsley
1 bouquet garni
½ cup whole black peppercorns
14 juniper berries, crushed
Coarse (Kosher) salt
9-pound leg of pork
¼ cup olive oil
¼ cup all-purpose flour
4 cups chicken or pork stock

Make the marinade: Combine the wine, vinegar, carrots, onions, garlic, bay leaves, parsley, bouquet garni, peppercorns, juniper berries and salt in a large nonreactive saucepan. Simmer for 5 minutes. Allow to cool. Score the fat on the pork to allow the marinade to penetrate. Put the pork in a large nonreactive container and add the marinade. If there is not enough to cover completely, add more wine. Cover and refrigerate for 1 to 2 days, turning occasionally.

Preheat the oven to 325°. Remove the meat from the marinade and pat dry. Place the marinade in a large pot and bring to a boil. Heat the oil in a large, heavy casserole. Add the pork and brown on all sides.

Remove the meat and set aside. Strain the marinade; discard the solids. Stir the flour into the hot oil and blend well. Place over moderate heat and gradually add some of the marinade, stirring until smooth. Add only enough stock to make a thick sauce. Return the meat to the pan. Cover and simmer over low heat for 3 to 4 hours, or until the pork comes away from the bone. Transfer to a heated serving dish.

Spoon off the excess fat. Pour the sauce into a small saucepan. Bring to a boil and cook until reduced slightly. Correct the seasonings. Pour the sauce over the sliced meat and pass any extra in a sauceboat. Serve with boiled potatoes, corn bread and a mess of greens garnished with grated hard-cooked eggs.

Serves 12

HAM AND CHICKEN PIE

Take a large silver serving spoon, break through the golden crust of what appears to be a plain chicken pie, scoop out a serving and reveal the secret at the bottom: a pie filled with pieces of country ham surrounded by a rich chicken cream sauce and savory vegetables. The combination of flavors is a soul-satisfying one and, with the addition of a good salad, constitutes a one-dish meal.

1½ cups cubed poached chicken
3 tablespoons butter
¼ cup all-purpose flour
1 cup chicken stock or broth
2 carrots, trimmed and minced
½ cup celery, minced
⅓ cup heavy cream
Pie dough for a 2-crust pie (page 60)
⅔ cup cubed or sliced ham (country ham is most flavorful)

Preheat the oven to 400°.
Heat the butter in the top of a double boiler over simmering water and stir in the flour. Add the chicken stock, carrots and celery and stir constantly until the sauce thickens. Stir in the cream. Add the chicken and cook until heated through.
Line a 1½ quart baking dish with half of the pie dough. Place the ham in the bottom and cover with the chicken and sauce. Cover with a top crust. Slit in several places to let steam escape. Bake for 25 to 30 minutes, or until the top is golden brown.

Serves 6 to 8

AUNT LIZZIE'S SALADE NIÇOISE

My Aunt Lizzie was a successful career businesswoman before there were many such around. She was a good-looking, stylish lady, always carefully groomed and smartly dressed. Aunt Lizzie knew and appreciated good food, but she couldn't cook for sour apples. "Woe to the day I can't afford to hire a cook," she used to say, gloomily contemplating starvation. Nevertheless, she loved to entertain and she set a fine table. One thing she did like to make herself was Salade Niçoise, which she had first tasted in France. The secret of making this salad successfully is using the freshest ingredients and taking care with presentation. Lizzie, with her strong visual sense and her perfectionist's instinct, could make a Salade Niçoise look like the rose window in a French cathedral. However, she had an aversion to the anchovies that are usually used. "They remind me of nightcrawlers in soy sauce," she said once. (Sorry to mention it.) So she always used slivered country ham to provide the salty ingredient in her composition. Asparagus is not part of the classic recipe either, but Aunt Lizzie used it in hers, arranged like wheel spokes. She liked to include nasturtium leaves in the greens for their peppery flavor and the blossoms, both beautiful and edible, for decoration.

3 cups green beans, blanched and chilled
3 or 4 tomatoes, quartered
1 cup Sauce Vinaigrette with herbs (page 34)
2 to 3 heads Kentucky Bibb lettuce, washed and dried
3 cups French Potato Salad (page 102)
2 cans (7 ounces each) solid white, water-packed tuna, drained
1 cup dry-cured black olives
4 ounces country ham, cut into ½-inch julienne
¼ cup drained capers
**2 to 3 tablespoons minced fresh green herbs and nasturtium
  leaves**
6 hard-cooked eggs, chilled, peeled and quartered
6 to 8 asparagus spears, cooked and chilled

Just before serving, coat the beans and tomatoes with some of the Sauce Vinaigrette. Toss the lettuce leaves in a salad bowl with ¼ cup of the vinaigrette and arrange the leaves around the edge of a large shallow bowl.

Mound the potato salad in the bottom of the bowl and decorate with the beans and the tomatoes, interspersing them with a design of tuna chunks, olives, ham slivers and capers. Pour the remaining dressing over the salad, sprinkle with the herbs and decorate the top with the eggs and asparagus.

Serves 10

WILTED LETTUCE

This salad, clearly of German origin, may have come into the Kentucky cuisine through the influence of the Amish communities located in Adair County. Like the Shakers, the Amish maintain a simple, old-fashioned life-style. Their recipes, like this one, reflect their origins in the German part of Switzerland. This salad is very good with boiled beef or with braises like Pork, Campbellsville-Style.

4 or 5 slices bacon
¼ cup mild white wine vinegar
1 teaspoon chopped fresh herbs
1 teaspoon grated onion (optional)
1 teaspoon sugar (optional)
2 heads Kentucky Bibb lettuce, or 1 large head Boston lettuce,
    separated and shredded
2 hard-cooked eggs, sliced, for garnish

In a skillet, fry the bacon until crisp; drain on paper towels and cut or crumble into small pieces. Heat the bacon drippings (or butter or oil) and add the vinegar and herbs to it. Add the crumbled bacon, onion and sugar.

Place the greens in a warm bowl and pour the hot dressing over them. Serve at once on warm plates. Garnish with hard-cooked sliced eggs.

Serves 4

GREEN PEPPER PUDDIN'

This dish is quite unusual; I have come across it only a couple of times in a lifetime of dining out, yet it is very simple to make, requiring only a little grinding and assembling. The resulting dish perfectly marries the zing of fresh green bell peppers with the richness of butter, eggs, cheese and cream.

4 large bell peppers, halved and seeded
2 cups coarse saltine cracker crumbs
2 cups grated sharp cheddar cheese
Freshly ground pepper
¼ cup (½ stick) butter
1¾ cups heavy cream
2 eggs, slightly beaten
½ teaspoon salt
1 teaspoon Worcestershire sauce

Preheat the oven to 350°. Grind the bell peppers and reserve both pulp and juice. (I prefer to grind the peppers in a hand-cranked meat grinder using the fine blade and to grind the crackers in the same grinder using the coarse blade. If you don't have such a grinder, a food processor may be used for the peppers but the consistency will not be as nice; take care not to reduce them to a purée.) Coarsely crush the crackers with a meat grinder or rolling pin. (Do not use prepackaged crumbs which will make your puddin' soggy.)

Generously butter a 1½ quart casserole or heatproof bowl. Fill the casserole, alternating layers of the cracker crumbs, peppers, pepper juice and cheese, seasoning with pepper and dotting with the butter and ending with a layer of cracker crumbs. Blend the cream with the eggs, salt and Worcestershire. Pour over the top. Bake for 45 minutes to 1 hour, until bubbly and browned on top.

Serves 6 to 8

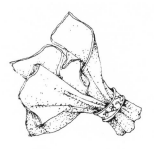

CORNMEAL BISCUITS

These will remind you of Scottish scones. They are a sort of coarse biscuit, only slightly risen. Split them while still warm and serve with plenty of butter and homemade preserves.

1½ cups all-purpose flour
¾ cup yellow cornmeal
2 tablespoons plus 1 teaspoon baking powder
1 tablespoon sugar
⅓ cup lard
¾ to 1 cup scalded milk

Preheat the oven to 400°. Sift together the dry ingredients. Cut in the lard with a pastry blender. Add enough milk to form a soft dough and knead briefly. Roll out ¼ inch thick on a floured board. Cut out with a 2-inch cookie or biscuit cutter or use a whiskey jigger. Bake for about 10 minutes, until risen and browned.

Makes about 2 dozen

CREAM OF TARTAR BISCUITS

These are my idea of the perfect biscuit, light, crunchy on the outside, flaky on the inside, rich with cream and golden brown. You can tell from reading the ingredients that there is a certain amount of art involved in making them; you have to develop a feel for the right ratio of flour to cream. Nevertheless, I urge you to experiment a little until you get to know when the dough is right, because once you have it you will never lose it and you can whip these up in no time. My Aunt Annie could make a batch for breakfast in 15 minutes, and 12 of those minutes were for baking, during which time she set the table and cooked the ham and eggs. And now her daughter, my cousin Helen, performs the same ritual and has time to work the *Courier-Journal* crossword puzzle, too.

2 heaping teaspoons fresh cream of tartar (see Note)
1 heaping teaspoon fresh baking soda (see Note)
2 cups all-purpose flour
1½ cups heavy cream

Preheat the oven to 475°. Sift together the cream of tartar, baking soda and the flour. Toss lightly with a mixing spoon to distribute the ingredients evenly.

Gradually stir in the cream, mixing gently as you do until the dough has reached a thick, lumpy but very moist consistency. Do not overmix. The final mixture should be similar to very thick, lumpy, sticky oatmeal. All this should be done quickly and lightly.

Sift some flour onto a wooden pastry board or table. Turn out the dough and roll in the flour to coat lightly. With a floured rolling pin, lightly roll out the dough ¾-inch thick.

Using a jigger or any 1½- to 2-inch cutter, cut out the biscuits. Cut close together so there is not much scrap dough left. As you cut biscuits place them close together, but not quite touching, on an ungreased baking sheet. Scraps can be gathered together and re-rolled but these biscuits will be less fluffy. Lightly prick each biscuit once in the center with a fork so the dough will lift a little (but not off the pan) and the biscuits will be light.

Bake for about 10 minutes or until a biscuit tests done when broken open. Serve hot.

NOTE: Both cream of tartar and baking soda lose their potency if kept too long after opening. Buy small quantities that you will use up quickly.

Makes 2½ to 3 dozen

Rhubarb

We used to have a patch of rhubarb growing in our kitchen garden. It had been there as long as anyone could remember, and it came up every spring on its own schedule without anyone doing much of anything about it. I remember James Miller Williams coming grinning into the kitchen on a bright early spring morning and the screen door slamming behind him as he announced, "Well, the pie plant's come up. Won't be long now 'til we get us some of that Roo-oo-oo-oo-barb pie." Somebody told me once that rhubarb was "blushing celery" so I tried to eat some raw, on the assumption that anything that tasted as good as cooked rhubarb must be wonderful just as is. Believe me, it isn't. It is sour, stringy and overwhelmingly puckery. Cooking and sugar are what make rhubarb edible. Nothing will make the leaves edible: They are full of oxalic acid and thus poisonous. There is even a little oxalic acid in the edible stalks, I believe, which is probably why aluminum pans change color if you cook rhubarb in them.

Enough of the chemistry lesson. Properly prepared, rhubarb is transformed from a frog into a prince and the necessary preparation is extremely simple.

RHUBARB PIE

This pie was always a favorite in our house and most other houses during rhubarb season. The crunchy, easily made topping contrasts nicely with the texture of the filling. You can add yet another texture by serving it with whipped cream.

FILLING:

3 cups diced rhubarb
¾ cup sugar
3 tablespoons all-purpose flour
1 unbaked 9-inch pie shell (page 60)

TOPPING:

½ cup wheat germ
½ cup rolled oats
½ cup all-purpose flour
½ cup sugar
½ teaspoon freshly grated nutmeg

½ teaspoon ground cinnamon
¼ teaspoon salt
2 to 3 tablespoons butter

Make the filling: Combine the rhubarb, sugar and flour. Mix well and spoon into the pie shell.

Preheat the oven to 375°. Make the topping: Combine all of the dry topping ingredients. Add the butter and mix in with a pastry blender. Sprinkle over the rhubarb. Bake for 35 to 40 minutes, until the topping begins to brown.

Serves 8

RHUBARB SAUCE

I like rhubarb tamed to about the level of a rather tart applesauce, at which stage it makes a fine foil for rich meats such as pork. Many people like it substantially sweeter and keep it chilled for use as a simple luncheon dessert or a snack treat. Either way you may like it better with a little lemon or orange zest added.

2 cups coarsely chopped rhubarb
½ cup packed brown sugar
Grated lemon or orange zest (optional)
½ cup golden raisins (optional)

Put the rhubarb in a nonreactive saucepan and sprinkle with the sugar. Add the citrus zest. Add enough water to keep the rhubarb from burning. Add the raisins. Cover and simmer until tender. Depending on the toughness of the rhubarb, this should take 8 to 20 minutes. Taste for sweetness.

Makes 1½ cups

Two Pie Crust Recipes

The way to judge a cook, my grandmother used to say, is by her pie crust. A proper crust is tender, brittle, well-flavored and flaky. I am including two pie crust recipes here using different ingredients and different techniques. One is a butter-based crust because many people think butter provides a better flavor. It is made with a food processor although, of course, the old-fashioned technique in the other recipe works just as well. Butter crusts stand up a little better than lard crusts so they are good for fruit fillings and free-standing tarts.

Lard crusts are flakier and more traditional. You may use vegetable shortening instead of lard if you prefer. You can do the initial blending of flour and shortening with a pastry blender, a food processor or, if you're an experienced traditional cook, your fingertips, but most of the latter probably don't need to read pie crust recipes.

With either recipe don't handle the dough more than necessary and don't let it get too warm.

BUTTER PIE CRUST

2½ cups all-purpose flour
⅛ teaspoon salt
¾ cup (1½ sticks) cold butter
⅓ cup ice water

In a food processor fitted with the steel blade, combine the flour and salt. Slice the butter into 1-inch cubes and drop into the bowl. Process until grainy. Add the ice water gradually through the feed tube until the dough forms a ball that runs around the edge of the processor bowl.

Divide the dough in half. Pat each portion into a disk. Wrap in waxed paper or plastic wrap and refrigerate for at least 30 minutes.

Flour a pastry board and rolling pin and roll out one disk of dough ⅛ inch thick. Fit into a 9- or 10-inch pie pan. Trim the edges and crimp decoratively.

Makes two 9- or 10-inch pie shells or one 9- or 10-inch pie shell with pastry for a top

LARD PIE CRUST

2¼ cups all-purpose flour
1 teaspoon salt
⅔ cup lard or vegetable shortening
¼ cup ice water

Sift the flour and salt into a mixing bowl. Add the lard and blend well using a pastry blender or a food processor. Add the ice water, stirring it in a little at a time with a fork. Flour your hands and roll the dough into a ball. Divide the dough in half. Press each half into a thick disk, wrap in plastic and refrigerate for at least 15 minutes.

Roll out one disk on a well-floured board ⅛ inch thick. Fit into a 9- or 10-inch pie pan. Trim the edges and crimp decoratively.

To prebake pie crust: Preheat the oven to 425°. Line the pie shell with foil. Fill it with aluminum pie weights, uncooked rice or beans to prevent bubbling. Bake for 6 minutes. Reduce the heat to 375°. Remove the foil and weights. Continue baking for another 5 to 12 minutes, until very lightly browned.

Makes two 9-inch prebaked pie shells or one 9- or 10-inch pie shell with pastry for a top

BUTTERMILK CAKE

Buttermilk is identified with Kentucky cooking just as bluegrass is with thoroughbreds. This example is an old family recipe from my great-great-grandmother, and it is wonderfully appropriate as a simple white wedding cake. The icing recipe is good on all kinds of things, but is especially pleasing on this cake.

1 cup (2 sticks) unsalted butter, at room temperature
2¾ cups sugar
4 cups all-purpose flour
1 teaspoon baking powder
10 egg whites, at room temperature, stiffly beaten
½ teaspoon baking soda dissolved in 2 teaspoons tepid water
1 cup buttermilk, at room temperature

Preheat the oven to 375°. Grease and flour four 9-inch round cake pans. In a bowl, cream together the butter and sugar. Sift the flour with the baking powder. Fold the beaten egg whites and flour alternately into the creamed mixture, reserving 1 cup of the flour. Combine the baking soda and buttermilk and pour into the batter just before folding in the reserved 1 cup flour.

Divide the batter among the cake pans. Bake for 25 minutes. Cool on a rack for 5 to 10 minutes. Run a knife around the edges to loosen from the pans and turn out on a rack to cool completely.

Spread each cake layer with Buttercream Icing (recipe follows) and assemble as a 4-layer cake. Decorate with fresh seasonal flowers.

BUTTERCREAM ICING:

3 cups (6 sticks) unsalted butter, at room temperature
6 cups confectioners' sugar
1 cup heavy cream
2 tablespoons vanilla extract
1 teaspoon salt

In a bowl, cream together the butter and sugar until fluffy. Gradually beat in the cream, vanilla and salt. Continue beating for at least 5 minutes until creamy.

Spread on the cake with a spatula and decorate using a pastry bag with decorative tips.

Serves 16

KENTUCKY COLONELS

There are many variations on these delicious traditional candies sometimes called Kentucky Colonels and sometimes called bourbon balls. Most of the recipes include chocolate, pecans and bourbon; beyond that the variations are endless, with some incorporating the chocolate in the ball of the candy, some, like this one, using it as an outer coating and a few dispensing with the chocolate altogether. They are a little tricky to make; it helps to have cool hands. A fine variation on this candy can be made by substituting crème de menthe; if you do so you may have colonels all right, but you can't really call them Kentucky Colonels.

1 cup (2 sticks) butter, softened
5 cups confectioners' sugar
Pinch of salt
½ cup plus 1 tablespoon bourbon whiskey or crème de menthe
1 cup finely chopped pecans
¼ cup light corn syrup
12 ounces semisweet chocolate

In a bowl, blend together the butter, sugar, salt and ½ cup of the bourbon. Add the pecans and corn syrup. Drop the candy from a spoon onto waxed paper. Refrigerate until firm, 20 to 30 minutes.

Melt the chocolate in the top of a double boiler over simmering, not boiling water, stirring with a wooden spoon. If desired, add the remaining 1 tablespoon of bourbon. Remove from the heat. Allow the temperature to register 96° on a candy thermometer.

Dust your hands with confectioners' sugar. Roll the candy into balls. Dip the balls into the chocolate to coat thoroughly. Place on waxed paper and refrigerate.

Makes 40 to 50

KENTUCKY FUNERAL CAKE

In Kentucky, and just about everywhere else I suppose, it is the custom to take foods to the home of a bereaved family so that they can eat and entertain friends without having to bother with cooking. It's a very nice custom and this cake is a good choice because of its versatility. It is actually an easy pound cake, made quickly and brought immediately to the home of someone who has died. It has the virtue of being good with all kinds of other sweet things, so it's handy to have around and you're not likely to get tired of it on funerary or other, less melancholy, occasions.

1 cup (2 sticks) butter, at room temperature
2 cups sugar
4 eggs
2⅔ cups all-purpose flour
1 tablespoon baking powder
1 cup milk
1 teaspoon salt
1½ teaspoons vanilla or almond extract

Preheat the oven to 400°. Butter a 9-inch springform pan. In a bowl, cream together the butter and sugar. One at a time, add the eggs and beat thoroughly.

Sift the flour with the baking powder. Fold into the creamed mixture. Fold in the milk and then the salt and vanilla. Pour into the prepared pan. Bake for 10 minutes. Reduce the oven temperature to 300° and bake for 40 minutes more, until a toothpick comes out clean. Cool on a rack for 5 to 10 minutes. Run a knife around the edge of the pan to loosen and invert onto a rack to cool completely.

Serves 12

Down-Home Cooking

*B*y "down-home cooking" I mean those foods casually served on a day-to-day basis back home. Almost all of these dishes are inexpensive and relatively easy to prepare, calling up the flavor of home to displaced natives of Kentucky and other parts of the South.

Many of these dishes, called "soul food," are the legacy of the black cooks of the past. Forced by circumstance to employ only the cheapest and least desirable foods, they learned to make silk purses from sows' ears, or at least to create true feasts from pigs' feet and vegetable tops. Their ingenuity in preparing the despised cuts of meat resulted in dishes such as fried chicken wings, often more sought-after than chicken breasts. Even chicken feet have found their way into soul food, and the only reason I haven't included a recipe for them is that I doubt most readers would be adventurous enough to try them.

The same attitude of "waste not, want not" also prevailed among most of the white population. Life on the frontier was hard, and thrift and frugality were unquestioned virtues, especially among the Scots who made up a large part of the pioneer population of Kentucky. When hogs were butchered, it was said that you could start eating at the Indiana end and eat every bit of it to the Tennessee end and still have the bristles left over for toothpicks. Sausages used every scrap of meat from butchering. When the last morsel was carved from a ham, the bone was used for pea or bean soup and the extra fat to flavor vegetable dishes or cooked greens or to grease a griddle for frying pancakes.

Things that today are considered waste material were saved and put to good use. Even the ashes from hardwood fires were saved and used in the form of lye, a necessary ingredient in converting corn into hominy. Lye went also into the production of homemade lye soap, a harsh cleaning agent that nevertheless produces the most beautiful white laundry you ever saw. Even more miraculous, unfortunately, is the ability of lye soap to make your wardrobe disappear, since fabrics washed in it tend to fall apart after a few launderings.

Ingredients for down-home cooking come from the woods as well as the fields. Fresh cress gathered from creeks, fiddlehead ferns, hickory nuts, dandelion greens are all found bounty. Wild tangles of thorny berry bushes—raspberry and blackberry—gave us as children a lesson in the inextricable intertwining of sweetness and pain in this life. We carried little tin buckets and came home covered in scratches and sticky berry juice.

Kentucky glitters with beautiful lakes, many of them man-made, and sport fishing is drawing more and more vacationers to the state. Fresh-water fish have always been a staple on the table back home, usually caught with low-tech equipment consisting of a bamboo pole, hook, line, bobber, sinker and patience. The fish were quickly cleaned and scaled and cooked very simply, coated with salt, pepper, cornmeal and a little flour and sautéed in hot bacon drippings in a cast-iron skillet.

Woodland mushrooms are a great delicacy and a good excuse for excursions into the woods. The ability to locate mushroom patches is a natural gift, like water dousing: either you have it or you don't. Good mushroom hunters were highly esteemed, at least in mushroom season, which started in spring and continued through fall, as different varieties magically appeared. There were also a few people, not necessarily good mushroom hunters, who were adept at distinguishing edible from poisonous mushrooms, a *very* valuable skill. My cousins and friends and I were always given stern lectures about poisonous mushrooms that had thrilling names like "death cap" and "destroying angel." To a child there is something about the idea that the innocent wicker basket in his or her hands may contain enough poison to wipe out half the town that perks up the day. There was never a chance to put one's monstrous capabilities to the test, however, because after we came home with our baskets of booty, they would be submitted to a mushroom expert (who took his or her fee from our harvest) to remove the questionable finds.

A few people made their living by gleanings from the woods. I remember one old woman, from one of the finest families in that part of the state, who lived in a cabin in the woods and came to town to sell the things she had gathered. She seemed to us, as children, to be witch-like and frightening. Nevertheless, our cook used to buy sassafras root and bark from her for sassafras tea and sarsaparilla. She was generally regarded as a harmless eccentric or "not quite right in the head," but as I look back in memory it seems to me that she would have been right at home if she had only been young in the 1960s.

There isn't much that is chic about down-home cooking, but if you develop a taste for it, it never leaves you. I encountered a party of Kentuckians in Paris a few years ago, rich, well-traveled and beautifully dressed. When I came upon them, they were dining in a great Parisian restaurant. After all the hoo-haw of greeting that marks these occasions, I asked how they were enjoying their meal. One of the women said, "Charles, it's heaven, just heaven! I've never had such a salmon mousse in my life. In the last three weeks we've eaten in most of the very best restaurants in France and each meal has been better than the last." She paused then and a thoughtful look came over her face. She lowered her voice a bit and said, "I wonder, Charles, do you happen to know of any place in Paris where you can get catfish and hush puppies?"

SASSAFRAS TEA

Sassafras (one of those words I can't spell without looking it up) is a tree that grows throughout Kentucky. From time out of mind people have been brewing the roots into a very pleasant herb tea.

If you've never tried it, you will be astonished at how familiar it tastes. That is because sassafras is one of the flavoring ingredients in root beer, also known as sarsaparilla. (I have to look that one up too, since in Kentucky we pronounce it SASSparilla.) The brewing of sassafras tea is said to have originated with the Indians, and sassafras root is regarded as having wonderful medicinal properties. I've heard that it will cure anything. That's what I've heard; what I've read is that it contains a substance that may be toxic if taken in very large quantities, so drink your sassafras tea, like your bourbon, in moderation.

1 cup cut-up sassafras root
2 quarts boiling water

Add the sassafras bits to the boiling water and continue to boil for 2 minutes. Turn off the heat and allow to steep for 5 to 10 minutes. Strain. Sweeten to taste with honey or sugar.

Serves 12 to 18

BLACK BEAN SOUP

Since childhood, I have loved this rich, warming soup, the perfect antidote to a cold gray day. Like all legume soups, it is a great stick-to-the-ribs food. It is slightly more elegant than some of the other bean soups since it is flavored with sherry as well as ham.

2½ cups dried black beans
1 ham bone with meat or ham hock
2 large onions, chopped
2 carrots, trimmed and chopped
3 celery ribs, chopped
4 to 5 parsley sprigs
6 whole cloves
Pinch of ground mace or allspice
Pinch of dried thyme
1 bay leaf
1 teaspoon dry mustard
¼ cup dry sherry
Thin lemon slices and sieved hard-cooked egg, for garnish

Soak the beans for 8 hours in cold water to cover.
Drain the beans. Place in a large saucepan or kettle with 2½ quarts of water and all of the other ingredients except the sherry

and garnish. Bring to a boil; reduce the heat and simmer gently for 2 hours, or until the beans are very tender.

Remove the ham and bone and 1 cup of the beans. Cut any meat into small pieces and set aside. Work the soup through a sieve or whirl in a blender or food processor. Add the reserved beans, diced ham and sherry and correct the seasonings. If you like, the soup can be served without puréeing it. Serve, garnished with lemon slices and hard-cooked egg.

Serves 8

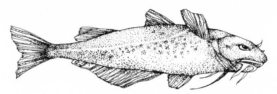

GREEN RIVER CATFISH WITH HUSH PUPPIES

For a long time if you mentioned enjoying catfish on the Eastern seaboard, you got the kind of reaction one might expect if you said your mother wore poke bonnets and smoked a corncob pipe. Nobody ate catfish. They look ugly and they sound worse. They have whiskers and they have to be skinned rather than scaled. Nevertheless, those of us who remembered the pleasure of eating catfish would have been glad to go right on eating catfish despite the social disdain, but for the fact that they were unobtainable except in places like Kentucky where you could catch them in local lakes and streams. In recent years, however, it has been discovered that catfish can be raised in shallow ponds constructed on farmland, and that catfish farming is a very efficient way to produce high-grade, delicious protein. Catfish, frozen and fresh, are now widely available in the North and people are learning what good eating they make. One of the best ways of preparing this firm, delicately flavored fish is one of the simplest, and most traditional—fried and served with hush puppies. The main rule is don't overcook the fish or it will become dry and rubbery.

FRIED CATFISH

6 fresh catfish, cleaned and filleted, if desired
1 teaspoon salt

1 teaspoon freshly ground pepper
¼ cup lard, bacon fat or shortening
¼ cup milk
2 eggs, beaten
1 cup yellow cornmeal

The fish should be thoroughly cleaned and drained. Sprinkle with the salt and pepper on both sides. In a large cast-iron skillet, heat the lard until sizzling. Mix the milk with the beaten eggs. Dip each fish first into the egg/milk mixture and then into the cornmeal. Fry the fish no longer than 3 minutes on each side. Serve with Hush Puppies (recipe follows).

Serves 6

HUSH PUPPIES

It is said that hush puppies originated when a large fishing party was fixing dinner on a riverbank. The dogs they had brought along surrounded the fire and set up a clamor of barking to get a sample of the catfish that were cooking there. To quiet them, someone rolled up balls of the corn bread dough, cooked them quickly in the skillet with the hot fat, and threw them to the barking dogs to quiet them. Thus the name.

Hush puppies are about crunch. Properly made, they consist of a brittle, dark brown crust surrounding a rich corn- and onion-flavored center. They crunch in the teeth and melt in the mouth and they serve as a welcome complement to the texture of the catfish they accompany.

1⅔ cups yellow cornmeal
⅓ cup all-purpose flour
2 teaspoons baking powder
1 teaspoon salt
½ cup milk
2 eggs, well beaten
1 large onion, minced or grated
Lard, for frying

Sift together the dry ingredients. Add the milk and ½ cup water. Stir in the eggs and onion. Add more milk if necessary to form a soft but workable dough. Using your hands, mold table-spoonfuls of dough into 1½- to 2-inch balls. Fry in about 1 inch of melted lard until well browned, about 2 minutes on each side. Drain on paper towels and serve very hot.

Makes 8 to 10 hush puppies

BARBECUED RIBS

Barbecued spareribs are always one of the most popular features at the big outdoor barbecues in Kentucky. A social club, a company, a church or just an expansive host or hostess will set up a striped refreshments tent, dig a fire pit or round up a line of cooks and charcoal grills in order to barbecue everything in sight, from a side of beef to a flock of chickens. No item is more in demand on these occasions than pork spareribs. I'm giving two ways of cooking them here: one for the outdoor grill and one for the oven, in case your prayers for clear weather have gone unanswered this time.

6 to 7 pounds of spareribs
2 tablespoons salt
1 cup cider vinegar mixed with 1 cup vegetable oil
Barbecue Sauce (recipe follows)

Charcoal Grill Method: Parboil the ribs before grilling for juiciest results. Rub the ribs with the salt and place skin side down on a hot barbecue grill over low-to-medium heat. Baste frequently with the combined vinegar and oil. After 30 minutes, turn the ribs and continue cooking, basting frequently. During the last 15 minutes of cooking, baste constantly with the barbecue sauce, or apply a good layer of barbecue sauce to the ribs and cover the grill with aluminum foil.

Oven Method: Preheat the oven to 425°. Parboil the ribs. Rub the ribs with the salt. Place skin side down on a rack in a roasting pan and brush with the oil and vinegar combination. Bake for 20 minutes, basting frequently. Lower the oven to 350°, switch to the barbecue sauce and bake for 30 to 35 minutes longer, continuing to baste. Serve additional barbecue sauce on the side.

Serves 6

BARBECUE SAUCE

Make the sauce in advance to have it on hand for basting. Since it can be kept in a jar in the refrigerator for long periods and since it is a general-purpose barbecue sauce suitable for either meat or fowl (especially roast duck), you might as well make a large batch by doubling or tripling this recipe for future cookouts.

3 tablespoons olive oil or light vegetable oil
1 small onion, minced
2 garlic cloves, minced
⅔ cup honey or molasses
½ cup chili sauce
½ cup ketchup
½ cup red wine vinegar
¼ cup Worcestershire sauce
2 teaspoons soy sauce
1½ teaspoons dry mustard
1 teaspoon ground cumin
1 teaspoon freshly ground black pepper
½ teaspoon dried oregano
Pinch of rosemary
4 or 5 drops of green or red hot pepper sauce, or a few flakes of dried crushed Italian red chili peppers

Heat the oil in a large saucepan. Sauté the onion and garlic until soft but not browned, about 5 minutes. Add all of the remaining ingredients and stir well. Bring to a boil, reduce the heat and simmer gently for 30 minutes.

Makes 2½ cups

CORNMEAL GRIDDLE CAKES

The use of cornmeal in place of the usual white flour or buckwheat makes these pancakes a welcome change. They retain the slight grittiness and distinctive flavor of cornmeal, but unlike the basic hoe cakes which are probably their remote ancestors, they are light and slightly risen by the action of baking powder. Serve them like any other pancake with the things you think make up a good pancake breakfast. Personally I'm partial to butter and sorghum for the griddle cakes and country sausage on the side.

1 cup white or yellow cornmeal
¼ cup boiling water
¼ cup all-purpose flour
⅔ teaspoon salt
1 cup milk
1 egg, lightly beaten
2½ teaspoons baking powder

Put the cornmeal in a bowl and pour in the boiling water. Let soak for 5 minutes and add the flour and salt. Combine the milk with the egg and stir into the softened cornmeal. Add the baking powder and stir vigorously. Heat and grease a griddle. Pour out just enough batter to make the size griddle cakes you prefer and turn when the top surface bubbles and the underside is properly browned.

Serves 4 to 6

FRIED CORN IN CREAM

At any but a very informal dinner, it is probably not a good idea to serve corn-on-the-cob. However, sweet corn in season is too good to pass up. This recipe uses that natural treasure and has the advantage of being eaten with a spoon. And it is wonderfully rich.

2 cups sweet corn, cut off the cob (see Note)
2 tablespoons butter, lard or fresh bacon fat
2 tablespoons chopped chives or green pepper (optional)
2 teaspoons sugar
1 teaspoon salt
¼ teaspoon freshly ground black pepper
About ⅔ cup heavy cream

Place the corn and butter in a heavy cast-iron skillet. Add the chives, sugar, salt and pepper. Pour in enough cream to cover the corn and cook slowly, stirring often, for 15 to 20 minutes, until thickened.

NOTE: Be sure to scrape the cobs to collect all the corn juices. In seasons when freshly picked corn is disappointing or unavailable, I substitute 2 packages of frozen corn, which is often higher quality than the corn-on-the-cob available in the market.

Serves 6

FRIED MUSH

Writing in 1643, Roger Williams described boiled mush in *A Key Into The Language of America* as "a kind of meale pottage, un-partch'd . . . beaten and boiled, and eaten hot or cold with milke or butter . . . and which is a dish exceeding wholesome for the English bodies." Be that as it may, most people don't take much interest in boiled mush, not realizing that it takes on a whole new dimension when you fry it. Indeed, whether your body is the English or the Transylvanian, I think you might be surprised to find that you love fried mush, which tastes like a superior version of your favorite packaged corn chips. And, as Roger said, it's wholesome.

1½ cups yellow or white cornmeal
1 teaspoon salt
2 cups cold water
1 egg yolk
1 cup milk
Fine cracker crumbs
Butter or bacon fat, for the skillet

Place 4 cups of water in the top of a double boiler and bring to a boil directly on the stove burner. Combine the cornmeal and salt and stir into the cold water. Gradually stir this mixture into the boiling water, a little at a time. Continuing to stir, cook over high heat for several minutes, until heated through. Cover and place over boiling water in the lower half of the double boiler.

Cook for 15 minutes, until thick. Pour into a buttered 9-inch square pan and cool until firm. (At this point the mush can be sliced and served as is. If it is not cooled, it can be served as a hot cereal at breakfast. It has more appeal, however, when fried.)

Slice the cooled mush into 3-inch squares. Beat the egg yolk with the milk. Dip the mush slices into the egg/milk mixture and then into the cracker crumbs to coat. Fry in a greased cast-iron skillet until golden brown. Serve hot, with honey, warm maple syrup or sorghum at breakfast, or serve plain with quail or venison as the Italians do. They call this dish "polenta."

Serves 6

FRIED TOMATOES

As far as I'm concerned there is nothing on earth more delicious than a ripe red tomato just off the vine, still warm from the sun, with nothing but a sprinkle of salt. But perfectly ripened tomatoes are not always available. Or, when they are available, they tend to come at you like a river in flood, so that a variation on that simple perfection can be very welcome. This recipe solves either problem. It masks the lack of savor in the slightly unripe tomato and it gives a change in flavor, texture and temperature to the overly abundant mid-season tomato crop. In addition, this recipe, made with green tomatoes, is equally delicious.

½ cup bacon fat
½ cup cornmeal
2 tablespoons all-purpose flour
1 teaspoon salt
1 teaspoon freshly ground pepper
4 medium ripe or green tomatoes, sliced

Heat half of the bacon fat in a heavy cast-iron skillet. Mix together the cornmeal, flour, salt and pepper. Dip half of the tomato slices into the mixture, coating both sides. Fry in the hot fat, until browned and crisp on both sides. Wipe out the pan and add the remaining fat before proceeding with the second batch.

Drain the tomatoes on paper towels. Serve hot on a heated platter as a condiment with breakfast or as a side dish with lunch or dinner.

Serves 6

PRESERVED GINGER PEARS

A gnarled old pear tree stood near the back door of my grand-mother's house. Four generations of my family grew up in that house, and I have the impression that all of them enjoyed pears from that tree. We loved the fresh fruit in season, and during the rest of the year, we loved the preserved ginger pears put up in late summer. As a condiment it, and other preserves like it, kept fruit on the table in winters before modern shipping and storage made fresh fruit available year-round. The product is so pleasing that people continue to make it even though it is now possible to wade knee-deep in strawberries and kiwi fruit in January. And I suspect they would continue to make it even if it didn't keep because it is so delicious as a foil for winter meat dishes.

9 pounds firm pears
6 cups sugar
Juice of 3 lemons
Grated zest of 2 lemons
½ cup chopped crystallized ginger
1 cinnamon stick (optional)

Pare, core and slice the pears. Put into a large nonreactive pot and stir in the sugar. Gradually bring to a boil, stirring until a syrup forms. Simmer, stirring occasionally, until the fruit is translucent. Add the lemon juice and lemon zest. Stir in the ginger and cinnamon. Simmer until the mixture thickens. Discard the cinnamon stick. Spoon the pears into hot, sterilized canning jars and seal with melted paraffin or canning tops while hot.

Makes 2 quarts

FRIED APPLES

Elizabeth Sanders, who gave me this recipe, always insisted that Jonathan apples are best for frying. However, almost ripe Granny Smiths or any other tart apples may be used if Jonathans are not available. The object is to use an apple that is sharp rather than sweet and that will not fall apart or turn mushy in cooking.

5 cooking apples
1 tablespoon lard, shortening or fresh bacon fat
1 tablespoon butter
1 cup sugar

Core, peel and slice the apples. Melt the lard with the butter over moderate heat in a heavy skillet, preferably cast iron. Add the apples, reduce the heat and cover the skillet. Stir the apples every minute or two until just starting to become tender. Add the sugar and cook, stirring, until the sugar melts and the apples brown slightly.

Serves 6

A Mess Of Greens

Beginning in late winter and early spring, fresh collard greens become available. These are followed by dandelion greens. Mustard greens are succeeded in late fall and early winter by kale and turnip greens. They are the leafy tops of a variety of plants—turnips, kale, collard greens, mustard, dandelions. All of these greens need to be eaten while still young and tender and all of them deteriorate rapidly after picking.

Some greens we bought from an old produce peddler with a truck farm outside town. Some came from our own garden. The dandelion greens came from the front lawn where, equipped with an old kitchen knife and a bucket, by a single act I simultaneously dug weeds out of the lawn and gathered food for the kitchen. At that period of my life I thought it wildly comic when grown-ups spoke about "a mess of greens" or "a mess of fish." Now, however, as a result of just looking it up in the dictionary, I know that the term is from the Old French word *mes*, meaning "meal," which is what the adults meant all along.

Greens are a good example of the way soul food evolved from a necessity in black kitchens to a delicacy in white kitchens. In the black community during the days of slavery there were few sources of vitamin-rich foods and, although nobody on earth had ever heard of a vitamin since they were not discovered until much later, age-old wisdom or instinct led mothers to seek out varied foods for their families. Greens are great natural sources for minerals and vitamins A and C. Kale and turnip greens served the same function for Eastern European peasants, since both were available in fall and winter when good vitamin sources were scarce. Indeed, kale is not usually eaten until after the first frost renders it milder and more tender.

All greens require careful washing to remove grit and all of them should have their tough stems removed. Most cooks tend to overcook greens, which is certainly in the cooking tradition. For example, in its original form the recipe for collard greens below called for a cooking time of 45 minutes. Overcooking, however, robs the greens of their nutrients and tends to make them strong-smelling. All of these greens tend to be pungent and highly flavored so they go well with pork and pork fat. They are good accompaniments to corn bread, fried chicken, pork and potatoes. The pot liquor can be drunk or added to soup stock.

TURNIP GREENS

Place washed, stemmed greens in a steamer basket in a stainless steel or enameled pot. Steam, covered, for 5 to 10 minutes, until just tender. Dress with butter or a little bacon fat or sprinkle with crumbled crisp bacon. Allow about ⅓ pound of greens per person.

DANDELION GREENS

These must be picked early in the season before the plants flower, or they will acquire the striking bitterness found in the milky sap of dandelion flowers. The very young leaves are a sprightly addition to salads. To cook dandelion greens, simmer them for 3 or 4 minutes with a bit of smoky bacon or salt pork. Drain, splash with a little vinegar and sprinkle with chopped, hard-cooked egg. Allow about ⅓ pound of greens per person.

COLLARD GREENS, MUSTARD GREENS AND KALE

2½ pounds of greens
1 pound bacon back, salt pork or cured ham hock
1 large onion
1 teaspoon cayenne pepper
1 teaspoon freshly ground black pepper
3 tablespoons salt (to taste)

Wash and drain the greens (you may use a mixture of greens if you like) and remove any tough stems. Place the meat and 8 cups of water in a large pot and bring to a boil. Stir in the greens, onion and peppers. Reduce the heat and simmer slowly for 15 to 20 minutes, until tender. Add the salt only after tasting because the bacon or ham will have added salt to the stock. Pass a cruet of vinegar at the table.

Serves 8

GLEATING'S POTATOES

These are thick-cut oven-fried potato sticks, easier to prepare than french fries and excellent with sausages or hamburgers. The name comes from the community of Gleatings, Kentucky, where my family had a farm and where these potatoes were a regular feature on the menu.

¼ cup corn oil or fresh bacon fat
3 to 4 large potatoes, cut into ½-inch strips with skin left on
⅓ cup butter
Salt and freshly ground white pepper

Preheat the oven to 350°. Heat the oil in a cast-iron skillet over high heat. Add the potatoes and brown on both sides. Spread the potato strips in 2 layers on a baking sheet or in a shallow baking dish. Dot with the butter.

Bake for 10-15 minutes, until tender. Drain on a paper towel and season with salt and pepper.

Serves 6

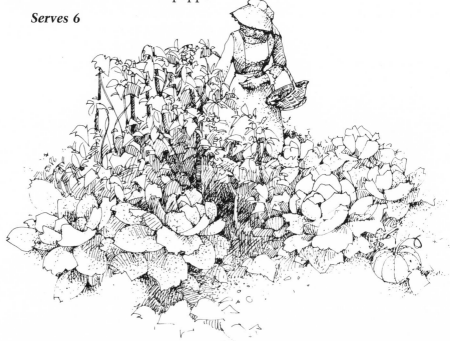

CABBAGE FIT-FOR-A-KING

Years ago on my first trip to Austria I had lunch in a very fine restaurant in Vienna. I was saving room for dessert because the waiters kept passing my table carrying the most beautiful cakes and pastries imaginable—endless fantasies of whipped cream, glacéed fruit, buttery icings and shaved chocolate curls—each more elaborate than the last. When the dessert menu was presented, I couldn't choose, not knowing enough of the language to know which was what. One item seemed like a sure bet, however. It was called *Kaiserschmarrn* and I at least knew that "Kaiser" means emperor. "Is it good, the *Kaiserschmarrn?*" I asked the waiter. "The late Emperor Franz Josef ate one every day," he replied. "If it was good enough for Franz Josef, it's good enough for me," I said imperiously. "Bring me *Kaiserschmarrn.*"

Kaiserschmarrn turned out to be a pancake with stewed prunes.

Some things said to be fit for a king, however, really are. The following recipe is not a dessert but it does surprisingly regal things for common cabbage, and I only wish Franz Josef were still around so we could try it out on him.

1 large head cabbage (about 2 pounds)
2 medium onions, minced
2 medium apples, peeled, cored and cut into ½ inch slices
¼ cup (½ stick) butter
1 teaspoon ground allspice
¾ teaspoon ground mace
1 teaspoon salt
Freshly ground black pepper

Shred or chop the cabbage and plunge it into a saucepan of boiling salted water. Cover the pan and boil for 5 minutes. Drain the cabbage and set aside.

In a large skillet, sauté the onions and apples in the butter until soft. Sprinkle with the allspice and mace. Add the cabbage and toss over low heat for 2 minutes. Season to taste with the salt and pepper. Transfer to a serving dish and serve.

Serves 6

SPOON BREAD

Spoon bread resembles other breads nutritionally, but not in consistency or flavor. The baking soda and beaten egg whites cause the spoon bread to puff up, and it turns a beautiful crusted golden brown in the oven. However, it is too moist to be sliced or even cut into servings; it must be spooned out, hence the name. The consistency is a cross between a pudding and a wet corn bread. It is served hot, buttered at the table and spread with preserves. Serve it with the same foods you would serve with corn bread, but as a more elegant substitute.

2½ cups hot milk
1 cup yellow cornmeal
1 teaspoon salt
¼ cup (½ stick) butter
1½ teaspoons baking soda
1 cup buttermilk
3 eggs, separated

Preheat the oven to 450°. In a saucepan, stir the hot milk into the cornmeal and salt until dissolved. Cook the mush mixture over moderate heat, stirring constantly, for about 5 minutes, until thick. Remove from the heat. Melt the butter in the bottom of a 2-quart ovenproof bowl or casserole. Dissolve the baking soda in the buttermilk.

In a bowl, beat the egg yolks. Add the buttermilk mixture to the yolks. Stir the mixture into the mush.

Beat the egg whites until soft peaks form. Gradually fold into the spoonbread. Turn into the prepared bowl or casserole. Bake for 10 minutes. Reduce the oven heat to 350°. Bake for 25 to 30 minutes, or until a fork comes out clean.

Serves 8 to 10

SHORTENIN' BREAD

I never think of shortenin' bread without remembering Nelson Eddy, a beefy baritone who was Jeanette MacDonald's co-star. A song called "Shortenin' Bread" was his musical signature and he delivered it in rich, enthusiastic tones embellished with an unbelievable amount of glee. The burden of the lyrics was that Mammy is about to make a little shortenin' bread and that Mammy's little baby, in the person of Mr. Eddy, loves shortenin' bread. All of this was a little hard to believe in that Mr. Eddy was the wrong age, the wrong size and the wrong color to be Mammy's little baby and very few babies sing baritone anyhow. Still, the enthusiasm was well founded. Shortenin' bread is simplicity itself to make, having only three ingredients, but it is a perfect accompaniment for tea or coffee or, if you happen to be Mammy's little baby, a glass of cold milk. As the name suggests, it somewhat resembles Scottish Shortbread.

½ cup (1 stick) unsalted butter or lard, at room temperature (see Note)
¼ cup packed light brown sugar
1½ cups all-purpose flour

Preheat the oven to 350°. Lightly butter a baking sheet. Cream the butter and gradually add the sugar while beating. Mix in the flour until thoroughly combined. On a floured board, roll out about ½ inch thick. Cut into 2-inch squares or use a cookie cutter. Place on the baking sheet for 20 to 25 minutes, until lightly browned.

NOTE: The use of lard is authentic, but then so is the use of butter and to my mind it produces a much superior result.

Serves 8

CRACKLIN' BREAD

Cracklings are the crisp brown bits of pork left after lard has been rendered. This fabulous bread was always made in the fall of the year, usually after hog killing time. For those of you who don't render your own lard, the recipe has been adapted to substitute cracklings made from salt pork. It is a wonderfully hearty bread served on a frosty evening after a day's work of harvesting. It's not bad after a day at the office, either, but if you aren't getting a harvester's quota of exercise you should probably go easy on this bread or you may find yourself selecting your suits from the "portly" rack.

The Italians make a somewhat similar pork-flavored bread incorporating prosciutto ham and pancetta bacon. I doubt this recipe is derived from that; each is simply the result of not being able to let good foodstuffs go to waste and making that necessity the mother of a wonderful culinary invention.

¾ cup finely diced salt pork or crumbled crisp bacon
2 cups cornmeal
1 teaspoon baking powder
1 teaspoon baking soda
½ teaspoon salt
3 eggs, well beaten
1 cup buttermilk

Preheat the oven to 425°. Render the salt pork over low heat until nicely browned. Drain the fat and save both the drippings and the cracklings. In a bowl, stir together the cornmeal, baking powder, baking soda and salt. In another bowl, combine the eggs, buttermilk and 2 tablespoons of the reserved drippings. Stir into the cornmeal mixture along with the cracklings. Pour the mixture into a well-greased cast-iron skillet. Bake for 25 to 35 minutes, until browned on top.

Serves 8

BUTTERMILK BISCUITS

These are probably what you think of when hot biscuits are mentioned. Light, moist and flaky, they have universal appeal. There is a recipe for Yeast Buttermilk Biscuits in "The Hunt," page 98. These biscuits also rely on the tang of buttermilk for their flavor but, because they employ baking powder for rising, they are simpler and quicker to make and thus are a fine hot bread for breakfast.

3 cups all-purpose flour
½ teaspoon salt
2 teaspoons baking powder
1 teaspoon baking soda
2 tablespoons shortening or lard
About 1 cup buttermilk

Preheat the oven to 450°. Measure all of the dry ingredients before sifting. In a bowl, sift together the flour, salt, baking powder and baking soda. Cut in the shortening with a pastry blender or 2 knives, or work in lightly with your fingers. Pour in just enough of the buttermilk to make a stiff dough. Stir until the dough pulls away from the sides of the mixing bowl.

Turn out on a lightly floured board and knead briefly until the dough is soft and spongy. Pat it out ½ inch thick and cut into rounds with a floured whiskey jigger or small biscuit cutter. Bake on an ungreased baking sheet until risen and lightly browned, 10 to 12 minutes.

Makes 3 dozen

SORGHUM AND BUTTER SPREAD

Sorghum probably came to the American colonies from Africa about 300 years ago, perhaps as a result of the slave trade. It is a form of cane-like grass. The leaves and grain served as forage for cattle and the cane is pressed for the wonderfully sweet syrup it yields. The most delicious sorghum in the world is made in Breckinridge and Hancock counties from sweet sorghum cane grown in that section of Kentucky. Good sorghum is rich and thick and has a distinctive strong flavor. It is readily available throughout the South but requires some detective work to find North of the Mason-Dixon Line.

⅓ cup butter, at room temperature
1 cup sorghum

Combine the softened butter with the sorghum in a mixing bowl. Work and beat with a heavy spoon until creamy. (If the sorghum is very thick it may be warmed slightly before adding to the butter.)

Serve with hot biscuits or cornmeal griddle cakes. The spread can be stored in the refrigerator for future use.

Makes about 1 cup

MOLASSES STACK CAKE

This is a very old-fashioned dessert with the molasses flavoring so familiar and beloved in an earlier America. The name, of course, derives from the stacking thin layers of cake interspersed with applesauce and covered with confectioners' sugar.

4 cups sifted all-purpose flour
1 teaspoon salt
2 teaspoons baking powder
½ teaspoon baking soda
¾ cup shortening
½ cup granulated sugar
½ cup packed brown sugar
1 cup molasses, sorghum or light molasses
3 eggs
1 cup buttermilk
2 cups applesauce
¼ cup confectioners' sugar

Preheat the oven to 350°. Butter and flour three 9-inch cake pans. On a sheet of waxed paper sift together the flour, salt, baking powder and baking soda. In a bowl, beat the shortening and add the granulated and brown sugars. Mix in the molasses. Beat in the eggs, one at a time. Stir in the flour mixture alternately with the buttermilk. Divide the batter among the cake pans. Bake for 15 to 20 minutes, or until the cakes pull away from the sides of the pans. Cool on a rack. Unmold and slice each layer horizontally into two thin layers. Stack the cake layers, spreading some of the applesauce between the layers. Sprinkle the confectioners' sugar on top.

Serves 8

SWEET POTATO PIE

Sweet potato pie looks and tastes something like pumpkin pie, since it employs many of the same flavoring ingredients. In texture, however, it is somewhat heavier and denser despite the addition of beaten egg whites. Because sweet potatoes can be harvested before pumpkins, this dessert shows up on Kentucky tables months before pumpkin pie is available.

1 cup mashed sweet potatoes
¼ cup granulated sugar
½ cup packed brown sugar

½ **teaspoon freshly grated nutmeg**
½ **teaspoon ground cinnamon**
½ **teaspoon ground allspice**
½ **cup finely chopped pecans**
½ **teaspoon salt**
2 **eggs, separated**
1 **teaspoon vanilla extract, or 3 tablespoons brandy or bourbon**
    whiskey
½ **cup (1 stick) butter, melted**
¾ **cup heavy cream at room temperature**
1 **unbaked single crust 9-inch pie shell (page 60)**

Preheat the oven to 350°. In a mixing bowl, combine the sweet potatoes, sugars, spices, pecans and salt. Beat the egg yolks and add them, along with the vanilla and melted butter. Mix thoroughly. Add the cream and stir well. Beat the egg whites until soft peaks form; fold into the batter. Fill shell and bake for 40 to 45 minutes, until set.

Serves 8

GREEN TOMATO PIE

This recipe might sound a little dubious, but if you don't think twice about making pies from very tart apples or lemons, why not green tomatoes? In fact, this pie tastes rather like rhubarb pie and, believe me, raw green tomatoes are a lot more edible than raw rhubarb.

We used to enjoy this sprightly pie during the entire tomato growing season, but especially in the autumn when it became clear that the tomatoes on the vine would not have enough time to ripen before the frost blighted them. Then urgency became the mother of action and we would gather baskets of green tomatoes to pickle for prudence and to bake into green tomato pies for pleasure.

½ **cup granulated sugar**
½ **cup packed brown sugar**
¼ **cup all-purpose flour**
½ **teaspoon salt**
1 **unbaked 9-inch pie shell with pastry for top (page 60)**
2 **to 3 tablespoons butter**
4 **cups thinly sliced green tomatoes**
1½ **tablespoons cider vinegar**
1 **tablespoon fresh lemon juice**

Preheat the oven to 375°. In a bowl, combine the sugars, flour and salt. Sprinkle half of the mixture on the bottom of the pie shell. Dot with the butter. Add the tomatoes and sprinkle with the vinegar and lemon juice. Top with the remaining flour mixture. Roll out the remaining pastry and cut into strips. Cover the pie with a lattice top. Bake for 50 minutes, until the crust is lightly browned.

Serves 8

BOILED COOKIES

These cookies are the only ones I've ever come across that are boiled and not thereafter baked. I know they sound a little peculiar but, after all, the Shakers had a recipe for boiled cake and the Shakers knew their way around a kitchen. Actually, the Shaker boiled cake got baked in the end. These cookies do not, but you will find them chewy and irresistible. They are better after standing for a day, and, if you prefer a crisp cookie, you may bake them for 8 to 10 minutes at 375°.

½ cup (1 stick) butter
4 cups sugar
½ cup unsweetened cocoa powder
1 cup milk
Pinch of salt
6 cups old-fashioned oats
1 cup shredded coconut
1 teaspoon vanilla extract
1 cup smooth peanut butter
1 cup chopped pecans

In a saucepan, combine butter, sugar, cocoa, milk and salt. Bring to a boil. Reduce the heat and simmer for 3 minutes. In another bowl, combine the oats, the coconut, vanilla, peanut butter and nuts and mix well. Add to the chocolate mixture and stir in. Drop by spoonfuls onto an ungreased cookie sheet and allow to cool.

Makes about 3 dozen

VINEGAR PIE

I assume that a sophisticated cook like you is not going to reject a fine, authentic old Kentucky dessert just because it sounds a little peculiar. You will notice if you read the recipe that there really isn't very much vinegar in it, and in any event, if the acid needed to make the recipe work were lemon juice, you wouldn't give it a second thought. This recipe dates from a time when vinegar was a lot more available in rural Kentucky than fresh lemons. Our ancestors on the frontier knew a lot about making do with what they had, often with very satisfying results, so give this recipe a try. You will be very pleasantly surprised.

FILLING:

4 egg yolks
1 cup sugar
3 tablespoons all-purpose flour
1 cup boiling water
2 tablespoons cider vinegar
2 tablespoons butter
Pinch of salt
½ teaspoon ground mace
1 prebaked 9-inch pie shell (page 60)

Preheat the oven to 325°. In the top of a double boiler, whisk the egg yolks. Add the sugar and flour and whisk until thick and lemon colored. Add the boiling water, vinegar and butter. Place over simmering water and cook, whisking constantly, until thick. Add the salt and mace and pour into the prebaked pie shell.

MERINGUE:

¼ teaspoon salt
¼ teaspoon cream of tartar
4 egg whites
6 tablespoons sugar

In a bowl, add the salt and cream of tartar to the egg whites and beat, adding the sugar 1 tablespoon at a time, until stiff. Spread the meringue on the pie, sealing the edges. Bake until browned, 35 to 40 minutes.

Serves 8

BROWN SUGAR PIE

Nobody calls anybody "Vinegar Pie," but "Sugar Pie" is a term of endearment that suggests sweetness, innocence and simplicity. It is used to address little children, and children are the greatest natural fans of this dessert. Don't, however, exclude adults with a strong sweet tooth from your list of potential customers for this perennial favorite.

5 tablespoons butter, at room temperature
2 cups packed brown sugar
3 whole eggs
3 tablespoons all-purpose flour
1½ cups heavy cream
1 unbaked 9-inch pie shell (page 60)

Preheat the oven to 350°. In a bowl, cream together the butter and sugar. Add the eggs, one at a time, beating well after each addition. Add the flour and cream. Pour into the pie shell. Bake for 30 to 40 minutes, until set.

Serves 8

OLD KENTUCKY ORANGE CHESS PIE

This recipe uses just the zest of the citrus rinds, but has the characteristic textural interest of a chess pie with its chewy top layer surmounting a custardy underlayer.

½ cup melted butter
1 cup sugar
3 eggs
1 tablespoon white cornmeal
2 tablespoons grated orange zest
2 teaspoons grated lemon zest
½ cup fresh orange juice
1 tablespoon fresh lemon juice
1 unbaked single-crust 9-inch pie shell (page 60)

Preheat the oven to 400°. Place the butter in a bowl. Add the sugar and mix well. One at a time, add the eggs, beating well after each addition. Stir in the cornmeal, zests and juices. Pour into the pie shell. Bake for 10 minutes. Reduce the heat to 325°. Bake until the filling just sets, 35 to 40 minutes more.

Serves 8

SCRIPTURE CAKE

The name of this cake is derived from the fact that all of the ingredients in it, even soda, are mentioned in one chapter or another of the Bible. (Butter is in Psalms 55:21; soda is in Galatians 5:9, etc.) This is the kind of novelty approach to cooking that one tends to distrust, but actually the cake is quite delicious. With figs and almonds for flavoring—what's not to like? It is dense and moist and, being rectangular and whitened with confectioners' sugar, it might be said to look like a page of scripture to the faithful eye. As you might suspect, this cake is very popular at church social events, being one of the few recipes available from the Ultimate Cooking Authority.

2 eggs
1 cup sugar
1 tablespoon butter
¼ cup all-purpose flour
½ teaspoon baking soda
¼ teaspoon salt
¾ cup chopped almonds
1 cup chopped fresh figs
1 teaspoon almond extract
Confectioners' sugar, for top of cake

Preheat the oven to 350°. Butter and flour a rectangular cake pan. In a bowl, beat the eggs until light. Add the sugar and butter and blend well. Sift together the flour, baking soda and salt. Add to the batter along with the almonds, figs and almond extract; mix well. Bake in the prepared pan for 25 to 30 minutes, until a toothpick inserted in the center comes out clean.

Sprinkle with confectioners' sugar to coat very well.

Serves 6 to 8

The Hunt

*I*n late fall after the harvest is in and well into winter, the great fox hunts take place. Carrying on a tradition begun in England centuries ago and still much subscribed to in Virginia, Maryland and Kentucky, red-coated ladies and gentlemen, mounted on fine hunting horses notable for their ability to jump, their stamina and sure-footedness, go careening across fields, fences and streams at breakneck speeds. They are madly, heedlessly pursuing a baying pack of specially bred fox hounds. The hounds are joyously, if confusedly, tailing a perfectly ordinary fox which, truth to tell, nobody much wants. The point of it all is the adventure, not the quarry, the journey, not the destination. The pleasures of fox hunting include the pageantry of the traditional dress and ceremony, the exhilarating thrill of speed and danger, the warmth of laughter and companionship and always the pleasure of satisfying a hunt-sharpened appetite with good food and drink.

All these joys, except the speed and danger, are also available in beagling, another form of fox hunt which doesn't require horses. This sport uses beagles rather than fox hounds, and the hunters follow them cross-country on foot. It is good exercise, a fine excuse for the complete round of hunt entertaining and quite unlikely to produce broken limbs.

The hunt is the centerpiece of the social event that begins on a frosty autumn morning with an elaborate sit-down breakfast. The Master of the Hounds presides at the head table with the guest of honor at his right. All the participating hunters are there, in addition to fair numbers of people who never ride to the hounds. I have seen one of the *grandes dames* of Kentucky in her scarlet hunting habit and derby, seated at the table of honor in the wheel-chair to which she was confined, her eyes sparkling like the diamond stickpin in her scarf.

The breakfast is an elaborate and hearty meal featuring such dishes as Fried Country Ham with Redeye Gravy, poached or scrambled eggs or Curried Eggs in Shrimp Sauce, smoked fish and oysters and perhaps smoked salmon flown in from Scotland, hot Yeast Buttermilk Biscuits with Blackberry Jam, Kentucky Bourbon Butter and perhaps a Sour Cream Coffee Cake.

This splendid meal is followed by the hunt itself, and when the weary but exhilarated riders return, a lavish cold buffet is spread for their refreshment with such dishes as Country Ham Salad Spread and French Potato Salad, Mutton Loaf with Fresh Mint Sauce and a variety of condiments including cucumber pickles, watermelon pickles and pepper relishes. And there will very likely be candied apples along with an assortment of such desserts as Burnt Sugar Cake, Pecan Tarts, Bourbon Pound Cake, Butterscotch Pie or Sponge Cake or Tipsy Cake. Everyone then returns home for a bath, a nap and a change into formal wear for the glittering hunt balls that follow at the Long Run Hunt Club in Louisville or the Grimes Mill Club House in Lexington, headquarters of the Iroquois Hunt and the Polo Club. The Beagle Ball at the River Valley Club in Harrod's Creek celebrates those hunters who follow the dogs on foot, and is one of the most elegant social events on the Kentucky calendar.

Now I suspect that you aren't planning to start a fox hunt of your own at this late date. Nevertheless, even if you're never Master of the Hounds except to your own cocker spaniel, you can learn some marvelous entertaining ideas from the dishes served by the fox hunters, most of whom combine the sophisticated palate of the socialite with the hearty appetite of the horseman. The American brunch appears to have its origins in the English hunt breakfast. And the tailgate party, which has become a fixture of the American football weekend, bears a considerable resemblance to the hunt buffet, although on a smaller scale. In fact, the customary hunt buffet is transformed annually into a lavish tailgate picnic on the occasion of the Hardscuffle Steeplechase, held each year on Squire Dinwiddie Lampton's farm. Mr. Lampton is famous for his fine coaches and the elegance of the women who ride in them. The Hardscuffle includes not only the steeplechase itself, but also hot-air balloons and an elaborate picnic under a tent or on the deck of the *Belle of Louisville*, the noted racing paddle-wheel steamboat. The day's events conclude triumphantly with a lavish tailgate buffet. Indeed, tailgate lunches using the recipes that follow or ones very like them are popular in the infield at Churchill Downs on Derby Day, at the point-to-point races held there every spring and fall and at Oxmoor, one of the oldest steeplechases in Kentucky, held every spring at the renowned Bullitt estate.

In short, for the informal weekend entertaining everyone loves today the traditional hunt festivities provide us with a versatile set of recipes that fit modern entertainment needs the way bourbon fits a julep cup.

FRIED COUNTRY HAM, REDEYE GRAVY

I don't know what you may think redeye gravy is, but your perception is probably colored by seeing too many movies in which cowboys belly up to the bar and growl, "Gi'me a glass of red-eye." What the bartender gives him presumably is a glass of raw whiskey, something like white lightnin'. That's what happens in those movies about the West called Westerns. If there were "Southerns," however, the cowpoke who ordered redeye (all one word, no hyphen) would get a coffee-based gravy for ham. He might be disappointed, but you shouldn't be. It couldn't be simpler to make and it's surprisingly harmonious with country ham. In fact, this dish is probably the simplest recipe in this book, and one of the best.

4 ham steaks, cut ¼ inch thick
1 cup water
1 cup black coffee

Heat a heavy cast-iron skillet until very hot. Grease it with a piece of ham fat cut from the steaks. Add the ham steaks and sear well on both sides. Add the water and cover the skillet tightly. Reduce the heat and let the ham simmer for 10 to 15 minutes, until tender. Remove the ham to a heated platter.

Increase the heat to high and add the coffee to the skillet. Cook, scraping with a wooden spoon, to deglaze the pan. Reduce the heat and simmer for 3 to 4 minutes to reduce the liquid a bit. Spoon over the ham and serve.

Serves 4

CURRIED EGGS IN SHRIMP SAUCE

This dish is a welcome addition to a hunt breakfast or brunch. It produces an almost uncontrollable urge to go out and pursue a fox or, if you're the sedentary type, to sit right down in an easy chair and read the Sunday paper.

CURRIED EGGS:

8 hard-cooked eggs, peeled
⅓ cup mayonnaise
½ teaspoon salt
½ teaspoon curry powder
½ teaspoon paprika
¼ teaspoon dry mustard

Cut the eggs in half lengthwise. Mash the yolks and mix with the mayonnaise and seasonings. Carefully fill the halves of the whites with the yolk mixture.

SHRIMP SAUCE:

2 tablespoons butter
¼ cup all-purpose flour
2 cups cream of shrimp soup (page 207, or see Note)
½ cup milk
½ cup grated sharp cheddar cheese
1 cup cooked peeled shrimp (optional)
1 cup fresh bread crumbs
1 tablespoon melted butter

Preheat the oven to 350°. In a saucepan, melt the butter and blend in the flour. Cook, stirring, for 3 minutes. Stir in the soup and milk. Cook, stirring constantly, until thickened. Add the cheese and stir until melted. Add the cooked shrimp.

Arrange the curried eggs in a 9-inch square baking dish. Cover with the sauce. Mix the bread crumbs with the melted butter and sprinkle around the edges of the dish. Bake for 20 minutes, or until the crumbs are golden brown.

NOTE: In a pinch, you can substitute one can of condensed cream of shrimp soup, diluted with one can of milk.

Serves 8

YEAST BUTTERMILK BISCUITS

Historically, Kentucky cooks used a great deal of the buttermilk that was the by-product of Kentucky's brisk river trade in butter. Today's cooks still use a lot of buttermilk because it gives baked goods such an interesting flavor.

The dough for these versatile biscuits can be made in advance and frozen for baking at the last minute. They bake up light and fluffy and are delicious either hot for brunch or cold at a picnic. I like them best served piping hot with butter and the blackberry jam (recipe follows) or as an accompaniment to Annie's Candied Apples (page 105).

½ cake of yeast, or 1 package (¼ ounce) active dry yeast
1 cup buttermilk
2 cups all-purpose flour
½ teaspoon salt
½ teaspoon baking soda

1 tablespoon sugar
¼ cup shortening or lard
¼ cup (½ stick) butter, melted

Dissolve the yeast in the buttermilk. Sift together the flour, salt, baking soda and sugar. Cut in the shortening until the mixture resembles coarse crumbs. Add the buttermilk all at once and stir until the dough pulls away from the sides of the bowl.

Turn out the dough and knead for 30 seconds. Roll out ½ to 1 inch thick. Brush with the melted butter and cut into rounds with a whiskey jigger. Place on a baking sheet and let rise for 1 hour or more in a warm place.

Preheat the oven to 450°. Bake for 15 to 20 minutes, or until the biscuits are lightly browned.

Makes 2 dozen

BLACKBERRY JAM

Blackberries grow in tangled brambles with lots of long, sharp thorns. I used to pick blackberries when I was a boy, so I'm in a position to state that anyone picking blackberries in a T-shirt is likely to wind up looking as if they tried to referee a cat fight. One of the privileges of being an adult is that I can now buy blackberries from June through August. Look for shiny, plump, deeply colored berries without caps.

2 pounds blackberries
4 cups sugar

Allow 2 cups of sugar for each pound of washed blackberries. Mix the blackberries and sugar well and let stand for 30 minutes. Mix again and set on the stove in a heavy cast-iron or stainless-steel pot. Cook, stirring constantly, over moderate heat until the jam is thick. Pour immediately into hot, sterilized mason jars and secure the sterilized jar tops.

Makes 4 pints

KENTUCKY BOURBON BUTTER

My mother's side of the family were all strict Baptist teetotalers, and my Grandmother Felts was a pillar of the Women's Christian Temperance Union. When I was six, she enrolled me in the L.T.L. (Little Temperance League), and I "took the pledge" never to drink. All of this caused some eyebrow-raising and ribald comment on my father's side of the family, since they were Presbyterians and not opposed, to put it kindly, to spiritous drink.

Even in Grandmother Felts' temperant Garden of Eden, however, there dwelt a serpent. She had a dear friend from Black Gnat, Kentucky, whom I'll call Beulah. Beulah was president of the local WCTU and a fervent and eloquent spokeswoman for total abstention. It was only years later that my grandmother learned to her horror that Beulah was the leading local bootlegger all during Prohibition. It seems that she had relatives back in the hills who operated a white lightnin' still for which she was the marketing agent. In addition, she had somehow obtained the inventory left when a small bourbon distiller went out of business at the beginning of Prohibition, and thus was able to provide customers with the smooth as well as the rough. "To add insult to injury," my grandmother used to say, "that old hypocrite used to give temperance lectures in the high school auditorium and then pocket the collection!"

I like to think of Beulah living her double life to the hilt. I sometimes imagine her in a powerful Winton touring car racing around back country roads in the dead of night, the revenuers in hot pursuit.

Bourbon butter is generally available on hunt buffets to spread on biscuits. You will also find it surprisingly delicious on hot pancakes or waffles.

1 cup (2 sticks) unsalted butter, at room temperature
⅔ cup confectioners' sugar
¼ cup bourbon whiskey

Place the butter in a bowl and beat in the sugar and bourbon. Scoop out dollops and place on waxed paper. Chill for casual shapes, or shape into a roll in waxed paper, chill and slice into disks. If you like, you can place the bourbon butter in a ramekin, smooth the top, chill slightly and garnish with a fresh mint leaf or a perfect strawberry. Can be frozen for longer than it's likely to remain uneaten.

Makes about 1½ cups

SOUR CREAM COFFEE CAKE

This delicious, buttery, nut-filled coffee cake has a texture rather like a moist, creamy pound cake. It's hard to identify sour cream in the finished product, but it gives the cake an elusive and pleasing distinction. Serve warm at brunch or at room temperature with coffee or tea.

CAKE:

½ cup (1 stick) butter
¾ cup sugar
1 teaspoon vanilla extract
3 eggs
2 cups all-purpose flour
1 teaspoon baking powder
1 teaspoon baking soda
1 cup sour cream

FILLING:

2 tablespoons butter
2 tablespoons brown sugar
2 teaspoons ground cinnamon
1 cup chopped pecans

Make the cake: Cream together the butter, sugar and vanilla. Add the eggs, 1 at a time, beating well after each addition. Sift together the flour, baking powder and baking soda. Add to the creamed mixture alternately with the sour cream and blend well after each addition.

Make the filling: Cream together the butter, brown sugar and cinnamon. Add the pecans and mix well.

Preheat the oven to 350°. Butter and lightly flour a 10-inch tube pan. Spread half of the batter in the pan and dot with half of the filling. Cover with the remaining batter and dot the top with the remaining filling. Bake for about 50 minutes, until a toothpick emerges clean. Cool on a rack for 10 minutes before unmolding.

Serves 8

CHEESE DELIGHTS

Cheese delights have a surprising combination of flavors and textures and provide something to munch on while having a cup of bourbon punch or a julep after the hunt. They are best served still hot from the oven but are also just fine at room temperature.

1 pound sharp cheddar cheese, grated
1 cup (2 sticks) butter, at room temperature
3 cups all-purpose flour, sifted
8 ounces pitted dates, cut into thirds
1 cup pecan halves
1 teaspoon cayenne pepper

Preheat the oven to 300°. Combine the cheese, butter and flour and knead into a ball. Place enough dough in the palm of your hand to make a flat disk about the size of a 50-cent piece. Wrap the dough around 1 piece of date and 1 pecan half. Sprinkle *very* lightly with cayenne pepper. Place on a baking sheet. Bake for 30 minutes, until lightly browned. Repeat until all the dough is used.

Makes about 3½ dozen

FRENCH POTATO SALAD

American potato salad usually consists of cold, cubed boiled potatoes mixed with flavorful vegetables (onions, celery, bell pepper, etc.) and bound with mayonnaise. In French potato salad, the potatoes are frequently flavored with wine or stock while still warm and absorbent, mixed with onions and/or other flavorings and moistened with vinaigrette. Mayonnaise, if used at all, is served on the side. Although this potato salad is made from an old recipe from Bardstown, Kentucky, the technique and ingredients are undeniably French. Bardstown was the home-in-exile of Louis Philippe, King of France, and I like to think that this recipe may have found its way into Bardstown kitchens when the Citizen King was in residence there.

8 to 10 medium new potatoes (about 2 pounds)
¼ cup dry white wine or dry vermouth
8 tablespoons olive oil or vegetable oil
¼ cup white wine vinegar, or 2 tablespoons vinegar mixed with
    2 tablespoons lemon juice

1½ teaspoons Dijon mustard
½ teaspoon salt
Freshly ground pepper
1 to 2 tablespoons minced shallots or scallions (optional)
1 to 2 tablespoons capers (optional)
2 to 3 tablespoons chopped mixed green herbs or minced parsley

Scrub the potatoes. Drop them into boiling salted water to cover and boil until just tender when pierced with a small knife, 15 to 20 minutes. Drain. As soon as they are cool enough to handle, peel and cut them into ½-inch slices. Place in a large bowl.

Pour the wine and 3 tablespoons of the olive oil over the warm potato slices; toss very gently. Set aside for a few minutes to absorb the liquids.

With a wire whisk, beat the vinegar with the mustard and salt in a small bowl until the salt dissolves. Gradually beat in the remaining 5 tablespoons of oil, adding it drop by drop at first. Season to taste with salt and pepper; stir in the shallots. Pour the dressing over the potatoes and toss gently to blend. Sprinkle the capers over the top and decorate with the mixed green herbs.

Serve warm or chilled.

Serves 6

COUNTRY HAM SALAD SPREAD

Nothing is superior to sweet butter and plain sliced country ham on crunchy beaten biscuits, but for a change (and to use up odds and ends of leftover ham), try this ham salad. Spread it on beaten biscuits, Melba toast rounds or dark pumpernickel bread.

2 cups finely ground country ham
2 cups finely diced celery
½ cup mayonnaise
¼ teaspoon freshly ground black pepper
¼ cup minced green bell pepper
¼ cup coarsely ground pecans
¼ cup minced onion

In a bowl, combine the ham, celery and mayonnaise. Cover and chill thoroughly. Just before serving add the black pepper, bell pepper, pecans and onion. Mix well.

Serves 6 to 8

MUTTON LOAF WITH FRESH MINT SAUCE

Mutton is not particularly popular in the United States, rarely appearing on the family dining table or restaurant menus. In Kentucky, however, the abiding influence of the British ancestry of much of the population has kept mutton popular, not only as family fare but as a dish proudly served at events ranging from fiestas to funerals. It shows up regularly at post-hunt buffets. Most people think mutton has a rather strong flavor and a dry texture. Kentuckians get around these objections by cooking mutton according to recipes that have stood the test of time. Roasted or broiled mutton is served pink and enhanced with garlic and herbs. Other mutton dishes, like this meat loaf, are kept moist by the addition of liquid (in this case, milk combined with cracker crumbs to absorb it), and are mellowed by the addition of savory ingredients. This mutton loaf cooks up firm but moist, and can be served hot or cold.

1 pound ground raw mutton or lamb (see Note)
⅔ cup cracker crumbs
1 cup milk
1 egg
1 green bell pepper, chopped (optional)
1 medium onion, chopped
1 garlic clove, crushed
1 teaspoon Worcestershire sauce (or more)
Salt and freshly ground pepper
¼ cup ketchup

Preheat the oven to 350°. Butter a standard loaf pan. In a large mixing bowl, combine all the ingredients except the ketchup and mix thoroughly. Form into a loaf and place in the loaf pan. Pour the ketchup on top. Bake for 1 hour, until cooked through and browned on top.

NOTE: If cooked meat is used, reduce the cooking time to 30 minutes at 400°.

Serves 6

FRESH MINT SAUCE

1 cup minced fresh mint
3 tablespoons boiling water
2 tablespoons sugar
3 tablespoons dry white wine or white wine vinegar

Place the mint in a gravy boat or pitcher and pour the boiling water over it. Let stand for 20 minutes for the mint to infuse the water. Add the sugar and wine, stir well and serve. This sauce may be served cold with leftover cold mutton loaf, if desired.

Makes about ¾ cup

PECAN TARTS

I expect you already know this Southern dessert favorite in the form of pecan pie, which is a splendid conclusion for a family dinner. Individual tarts are easier to serve at a buffet, however, and have more style. Whipped cream is a delightful accompaniment to the tarts, as it is to pecan pie.

10 unbaked 2-inch tart shells, made with one of the pie crust
    recipes on page 60
4 eggs
½ cup packed brown sugar
¾ cup light corn syrup
⅛ teaspoon salt
1 teaspoon vanilla extract
¼ cup melted butter
1 cup pecan halves

Preheat the oven to 400°. Bake the tart shells for about 5 minutes to set the pastry. Reduce the oven temperature to 300°.

In a bowl, beat the eggs until frothy. Add the brown sugar, corn syrup, salt, vanilla, melted butter and pecans. Stir well and divide among the tart shells. Bake for 10 minutes, or until a knife inserted in the center of the filling comes out clean.

Serves 10

ANNIE'S CANDIED APPLES

This very special dish is well known in Kentucky. I first tasted it when I was a child at the breakfast table of a favorite aunt, who presented it as a heavy preserve, with homemade cream of tartar biscuits that would melt in your mouth. After years of trying to duplicate this dish, I now realize that there is a great art in preparing it, and that it has to be done in just the right way. I recommend using an extra-large, covered, heavy kettle or pot to allow for proper heat distribution. I also recommend Winesap apples because they have a texture that holds up in the cooking process without getting mushy.

½ cup (1 stick) plus 1 tablespoon butter
6 to 8 Winesap apples, cored, peeled and halved
2 tablespoons fresh lemon juice
1 cup sugar (see Note)
½ teaspoon ground cinnamon
¼ teaspoon freshly grated nutmeg

Grease a large kettle or heavy pot with the 1 tablespoon butter. Add the apples. Sprinkle with the lemon juice. Add the sugar, the remaining ½ cup butter and ¼ cup water. Sprinkle with the cinnamon and nutmeg. Bring to a full boil, cover and reduce the heat to a simmer. Simmer the apples for 35 minutes *without removing the cover*.

NOTE: You may substitute ½ cup packed brown sugar for the white sugar; this will produce a caramelized effect on the apples.

This recipe may be baked in an uncovered casserole in a 300° oven for 45 minutes, but the consistency of the apples will not be as firm as with the kettle method.

Serves 6

BURNT SUGAR CAKE

This cake is somewhat whimsically named. Both the cake and the icing are suffused with the rich flavor of caramel, and of course the whole trick in making caramel is to keep a sharp eye on it to prevent it from burning. Nevertheless, the original recipe refers to the caramel as burnt sugar throughout, apparently assuming that anyone but a damn fool would know you shouldn't actually burn it.

CAKE

1¾ cup sugar
1 cup boiling water

½ cup (1 stick) butter
2 eggs, beaten
1 cup buttermilk
1 teaspoon vanilla extract
3 cups all-purpose flour
¾ teaspoon baking soda
1 teaspoon baking powder

Make the cake: Preheat the oven to 350°. Butter two 9-inch round cake pans. In an iron skillet, cook 1 cup of the sugar until dark brown in color (being careful not to let it burn). Very carefully add the boiling water (the mixture will bubble up) and cook for 5 minutes to form a rich, dark syrup. Set aside to cool.

Cream the butter with the remaining ¾ cup sugar. Add the eggs. Add the buttermilk and vanilla and mix well.

In a large mixing bowl, sift the flour. Add the baking soda and baking powder. Add slowly to the creamed mixture. Gradually fold in ⅔ cup of the cooled burnt sugar mixture; reserve the remainder for the icing. Divide the batter between the cake pans. Bake for 35 to 40 minutes, or until a cake tester inserted in the center of the cake comes out clean. Cool on a rack for 5 to 10 minutes. Run a knife around the edge of the pans to loosen and invert onto a rack to cool.

ICING:

2 cups sugar
½ cup (1 stick) butter
1 cup milk
3 tablespoons reserved burnt sugar syrup

In a heavy saucepan, combine the sugar, butter, milk and burnt sugar syrup. Bring to a boil over low heat and cook to 238° to 240°, between the soft and firm ball stages, or until it almost forms a firm ball when tested in cold water. Remove from the heat and allow to cool to lukewarm. Beat until creamy. Spread the bottom cake layer with the icing. Position the top layer above it and frost the top and sides with the remaining icing.

Serves 12

BUTTERSCOTCH PIE

My cousin Helen was as famous for her Butterscotch Pie as her mother, my aunt Annie, was for Chess Pie (page 137). One of my earliest memories is of hanging around the kitchen with my mouth watering as each prepared her respective specialty. This is how Helen did it.

2 tablespoons butter
1 tablespoon all-purpose flour
1 cup packed brown sugar
1½ cups milk
4 eggs, separated
1 unbaked 9-inch pie shell (page 60)
¼ cup plus 2 tablespoons granulated sugar
½ teaspoon vanilla extract

Preheat the oven to 375°. In a saucepan, cook the butter until browned. Add the flour, brown sugar, milk and beaten egg yolks. Mix well. Cook over low heat until thick. Pour into the pie shell. Bake until the crust is browned and the filling is set, 20 to 25 minutes.

Meanwhile, make the meringue: Beat the egg whites until they form stiff peaks. Gradually fold in the granulated sugar and the vanilla. Smooth the meringue over the top of the pie, making sure it slightly overlaps the edges of the pie crust to prevent shrinkage. Bake for 5 minutes, to lightly brown the meringue.

Serves 8

SPONGE CAKE

A light, moist sponge cake is superbly versatile. This one, fragrant with citrus, can be used as the base for the Tipsy Cake recipe that follows, iced with your favorite frosting or served very simply covered with a cake glaze.

1 teaspoon grated orange or lemon zest
1 cup sifted sugar
6 eggs, separated and at room temperature
¼ cup boiling water or hot coffee
1 tablespoon fresh lemon juice or vanilla extract, or several
    drops anise oil
1 cup cake flour
1½ teaspoons baking powder
¼ teaspoon salt

Preheat the oven to 350°. Stir the grated zest into the sugar. In a bowl, beat the egg yolks until light and foamy. Gradually add the sugar and continue to beat until the mixture is pale and thick. It has reached the proper consistency when a sample dropped from a spoon remains for a moment above the rest of the batter and then settles down rather slowly to the level in the bowl.

Beat in the boiling water until cool. Beat in the lemon juice. Sift the cake flour, then resift it with the baking powder and salt. Add the sifted ingredients gradually to the yolk mixture, folding until blended.

Beat the egg whites until stiff but not dry. Fold lightly into the batter. Spoon the batter gently into a scrupulously clean tube cake pan with a removable rim (the central tube helps support the dough while it rises, but any grease remaining in the pan will prevent the batter from rising). Bake for about 45 minutes, until a toothpick emerges clean.

When the cake is done, invert the tube pan over a funnel or the neck of a bottle, keeping the cake above the surface of the table. Let the cake hang for about 1½ hours, until thoroughly set. Remove from the pan before storing.

Serves 6 to 8

TIPSY CAKE

One of my cousins would occasionally get a little giddy on festive occasions when juleps, wine and cordials accompanied dinner, but she always insisted that it was the alcohol in the food, not the drinks she allowed herself, that went to her head. I always felt a little skeptical about her explanation, but when this cake is on the menu she could be right. This dessert isn't cooked after the sherry is added, and sponge cake soaks up wine like—well, like a sponge. With the custard, nuts and whipped cream it's a luscious dessert, but don't eat more than one serving if you're driving or operating heavy machinery.

Sponge Cake (see preceding recipe), cut into large cubes
2 cups whole almonds
1¾ cups sweet sherry
4 cups Boiled Custard (page 191)
3 cups heavy cream, whipped

Stud each cake cube with an almond, pushing it all the way into the cake. Place the cubes in a glass bowl. Slowly pour the sherry over the cake cubes, allowing it to be thoroughly absorbed.

Pour the cooled custard over the cake to coat and cover. Refrigerate for 8 hours or more. Serve topped completely with the whipped cream.

Serves 16 to 24

BOURBON POUND CAKE

This is a dense, moist cake rather like a fruitcake without the fruit that improves with age if it is well wrapped in foil and stored in the refrigerator. Do not freeze it. Usually served plain, bourbon pound cake is also delicious with Hard Sauce, page 201.

1½ cups (3 sticks) butter, at room temperature
2 cups granulated sugar
2 cups packed light brown sugar
8 eggs
5 cups sifted all-purpose flour
¼ teaspoon salt
1 teaspoon ground mace
1½ cups bourbon whiskey
2 cups pecan meats, broken into medium-size pieces

Cream the butter until soft in a large mixing bowl. Combine the sugars. Gradually work 2 cups of the mixed sugars into the creamed butter, beating until smooth.

In another bowl, beat the eggs until frothy. Gradually beat in the remaining 2 cups sugar until smooth and creamy. Pour the egg mixture into the creamed butter and mix.

Preheat the oven to 300°. Butter a 10-inch tube pan. Sift together the flour, salt and mace. Add the flour mixture to the batter alternately with the bourbon, beginning and ending with the flour. Stir in the pecans.

Pour the batter into the prepared pan, almost filling it. Bake for 1½ to 1¾ hours, or until the cake shrinks back slightly from the sides. Cool the cake in the pan for about 15 minutes. Turn out and cool completely on a cake rack. ***Serves 16 to 20***

DIVINITY CANDY

Divinity, occasionally called Divinity Fudge, is a sweet, slightly soft, vanilla-flavored candy studded with nuts. The only tricky thing about it is getting the temperature of the cooking candy syrup to the right level before adding it to the egg whites. If you have a candy thermometer this is easy enough to do, but when I was growing up I never heard of a candy thermometer and I never knew anyone to use one. We tested, as you can do, by dropping a teaspoon of the mixture into a glass of cold water. If it forms a ball, press it lightly, and if it has become firm but slightly pliable the candy has cooked enough.

3 cups sugar
¾ cup light corn syrup
3 egg whites
1 teaspoon vanilla extract
½ cup chopped pecans

In a heavy saucepan, combine the sugar, corn syrup and ½ cup water. Cook, without stirring, until the mixture reaches the hard ball stage, 248° to 250° on a candy thermometer.

Meanwhile, beat the egg whites until stiff. Beating at high speed, slowly pour the hot syrup over the beaten egg whites. Add the vanilla and continue to beat until the mixture forms soft peaks and begins to lose its gloss. Stir in the pecans.

Drop the candy in dollops onto waxed paper and wrap well.

Makes 2 dozen candies

The Harvest And Thanksgiving

$\mathcal{K}$entucky's annual state and county fairs mark the turn of the season from the late summer harvest of sweet corn, tomatoes, squash, cucumbers, beets and hay to the autumn harvesting and gleaning of grain crops, pumpkins, late apples and tobacco, the state's biggest cash crop. The fairs occur when heroic-size vegetables have reached full growth, food animals have fattened for judging and the great draft horses are in prime condition for the log-pulling competition. There are invariably races for man and beast, greased-pole climbing contests, baton twirlings, pie-eating contests, judgings and whoop-de-do of all kinds, but for cooks and eaters the main event is the awarding of blue ribbons for all kinds of cooking and baking.

Under striped tents or in permanent fairgrounds buildings the air is filled with the golden flecks of dust motes caught by the late summer sun, and with thrilling aromas of pies made with the fruits of the season—blueberry and blackberry, apple, peach, quince, plum, pear—or from anything else that makes a good pie—pecan, coconut, chocolate, custard, walnut, sweet potato, pumpkin, tomato, mincemeat and so on. And there are rows and rows of Mason jars filled with preserves, glowing with brilliant colors, each bearing a carefully lettered card with the name of the proud cook who submitted it. The judges gravely sample the contents of each jar, taking little bites in order not to overwhelm their judicial palates and so lose all interest in the outcome.

The cakes tend to be elaborate and the competition intense. I remember two old friends, Hattie and Bertha, who stopped speaking to one another after the bake-off one year. Bertha had wheedled an old family cake recipe out of Hattie, saying she wanted to bake it as a birthday cake for one of her children. Hattie had been fixing to win the ribbon herself that year, and she was fit to be tied when Bertha showed up with a familiar-looking cake and took the blue ribbon with it. Hattie was heard to say afterwards, "That was my own Aunt Ula's fancy cake receipt she used. I wouldn't so much mind if she'd just done something like run off with my husband, but it's like as if she not only run off with my husband but stole my best dress to do it in!"

When I once asked our cook, Anna Smith, why she always tasted the raw cake batter for her entry for the Taylor County Fair baking competition before she put it in the oven, she said everyone in town did that ever since one woman sabotaged her rival by sneaking into her kitchen the day before the fair (nobody in small-town Kentucky locks the door) and mixing salt in the sugar canister. I don't know whether the saboteur won, but her victim certainly didn't. Pillsbury Bake-offs have bigger prizes, but they don't produce good feuds like county fairs do.

When the first cold weather occurs after the harvest, usually along about Thanksgiving time, the country people kill and butcher some of their livestock and prepare it for winter consumption. The animals are in prime condition after summer feeding, the farmers want to avoid having to provide fodder over the winter, and the cool weather of the late fall or early winter retards spoilage of the freshly butchered meat. This slaughtering process has been going on from time immemorial; it is necessary but a little unsettling if you're not used to it, and since this is a cookbook and intended to whet, not kill, your appetite, we will now skip lightly past the butchering and consider the preparation and preservation of the meat.

There are now cold storage and freezing lockers available in rural areas, so that turning beef into dried or corned beef and salting and smoking pork is no longer a necessity. Just the same, the old methods of preservation—salting, drying, pickling and smoking—are all still used not just to preserve meats but to achieve the flavors and textures that people have come to love. Indeed, modern food manufacturers who have no need or inclination to go to the trouble and expense to wood-smoke hams, bacon and sausages often imitate the flavor of the traditional preservation process with artificial smoke flavoring. I'm here to tell you it isn't quite the same: "Not nohow!", as Kentuckians say for emphasis.

Of all the holidays, the Thanksgiving celebration of the harvest is to me the most evocative of our beginnings as a nation. Thanksgiving is one of those few entirely American institutions dating back over respectable stretches of historic time: The Pilgrims landed at Plymouth Rock on November 21, 1620. Now I suspect that most cookbook authors (certainly this one) are fond of comfort, warmth, good cheer and, where possible, a little luxury. I suspect most cookbook readers are the same. But if anything was in short supply in November 1620, it must have been comfort, warmth, cheerfulness and luxury. I don't know whether you have ever seen the New England coast in late November: It has a certain austere beauty, stern and forbidding, but it is not inviting. Stepping off the Mayflower that day onto the bleak shores of the New World with the winter ahead must have taken courage and determination of a very high order. I sometimes wonder what the Pilgrims and an ancestor of mine among them must have thought as they made their way across the beach. Gratitude, undoubtedly, for having arrived safely, and a sense of release in getting off a small ship crammed to the gunwales with people, baggage and domestic animals. Mingled with the relief, however, must have been apprehension and foreboding about what was to come. They must have resolved that if they could just get through the next year they would give thanks to their God and try to make up to themselves a little for that bleak arrival. It's the sort of promise you make to yourself to keep up your courage and determination, like Scarlett O'Hara's resolve, "As God is my witness, I'm never going to be hungry again."

A year later they kept their promise with a feast, the first

Thanksgiving. Central to the menu were two foods not to be found in the Old World—wild turkeys and corn—along with some familiar foods such as venison and the oysters the settlers were delighted to find in teeming abundance on the shores of this new land.

We are still keeping the promise the Pilgrims made in 1620 to give thanks, and we preserve that memory in part by serving many of the same foods. The Kentucky Thanksgiving feast offered in this chapter is built around distinctively American foods. Our menu starts with Acorn Squash Soup or Butternut Squash Soup with Apples. The main course is roast turkey, of course: This is one feast in which it seems plain perverse to break with tradition, since turkey is so good. It would be nice to use wild turkey for its historic connotations as well as its subtle gamy flavor, but the elusive creatures are very rare now. We will be more than content with a modern domestic bird, practically spherical in shape with an enormous breast, compared to which the wild turkey seems wiry and scrawny. Our turkey is stuffed with a dressing made from corn bread. We will also serve giblet gravy and seasonal vegetables, and the table will be enlivened by an assortment of relishes in contrasting colors, textures and flavors from the bounty of the recent harvest. And, this being Kentucky, we will pass a platter of very thinly sliced aged country ham as an accompaniment rather than a course; its dry texture and nutty flavor serve as a nice foil for the succulence of the turkey. Dessert will be Lonzetta's Pumpkin, Chess or Shaker Lemon Pie, along with Pecan Bourbon Cake and Creamy Pralines.

So let us now prepare some of the food rewards of the season from no-longer-summer to almost-winter.

Two Squash Soups

Butternut and acorn squashes, the main ingredients in these lush, subtly flavored soups, ripen in late summer and remain available late into the winter. Either soup can be made with other squash, including even pumpkin, but acorn and butternut work especially well. The first soup plays off the natural sweetness of the squash with a garnish of toasted pecans. The second enhances this sweetness with the addition of fall apples.

ACORN SQUASH SOUP

2 cups acorn squash purée
Salt and freshly ground pepper
1½ cups heavy cream
3½ cups chicken stock
½ cup chopped toasted pecans
Freshly grated nutmeg

In a large saucepan, season the purée with salt and pepper to taste. Stir in 1 cup of the cream and the chicken stock. Bring just to a boil, stirring occasionally. Whip the remaining ½ cup heavy cream. Serve hot, garnished with the whipped cream and the chopped toasted pecans. Dust with freshly grated nutmeg or pass the nutmeg grater with the soup.

Serves 6

BUTTERNUT SQUASH SOUP WITH APPLES

2 pounds butternut squash, peeled, seeded and cubed
2 McIntosh apples, peeled and cored, plus 1 McIntosh apple
     with the peel, thinly sliced
5 cups chicken stock
½ teaspoon salt
¼ teaspoon freshly ground white pepper
¼ teaspoon ground mace
2 tablespoons fresh lemon juice
1½ cups heavy cream

Cook the squash and the 2 peeled apples in 4 cups of the chicken stock for 10 minutes. Put in a blender or food processor with the remaining 1 cup chicken stock and purée until smooth. Strain through a sieve, purée a second time and strain again. Place the mixture in a saucepan and bring to a boil. Season with the salt, pepper and mace; add the lemon juice and mix thoroughly. Add 1 cup of the heavy cream and bring to just below the boiling point over low heat. Whip the remaining ½ cup heavy cream.

Ladle the soup into individual bowls and garnish with dollops of the whipped cream and apple slices.

Serves 8

Country Sausage

Hog butchering, which takes place every year at the onset of cold weather, is inextricably linked to sausage making. Mankind learned thousands of years ago the wisdom we know as "Waste not, want not." Since earliest times, there has been an iron necessity to use every useful part of valuable animals—skins for garments, bones for tools, tendons for thongs, intestines for bow strings or whatever. If a group of neolithic hunters were standing around the carcass of a freshly killed wild boar (in those days all boars were wild), we can be sure that they were all members of the clean plate club, ever mindful of their old mothers' admonitions to use "everything but the squeal." Of course there was never any problem about what to do with the pork chops or the hams or the pork tenderloin. The difficulty was all those odd bits, pieces and scraps left over. I'm not sure how they solved the problem, but given the social conventions of the day, they probably handed the miscellany over to their mates and expected them to be suitably grateful. After eons of this sort of thing people eventually learned to grind up the odds and ends left over after butchering, to combine them with herbs, spices and salt for preservation, to stuff them into lengths of cleaned intestines and sometimes to dry or smoke them and to call the resulting product "sausage." Not all sausages, of course, are made of pork. There are beef and veal sausages as well as deer sausages and, I suspect, yak sausages, hippopotamus sausages and, come to think of it, seafood sausages—a delicacy in many a nouvelle cuisine restaurant.

Almost every part of the world produces sausages and, as you might expect, the varieties are endless. Some are made from coarsely ground meat, like the Italian sweet sausages, others from puréed meat, like frankfurters. Some are highly spiced like chorizo, a Spanish variety. Others are mild to bland, like the German weisswurst. They come hard and dry like pepperoni or summer sausage which can be stored for long periods without refrigeration. Or they can be partially cured, pre-cooked and stored for reasonable periods in the refrigerator. Or they may be fresh sausages, which must be eaten almost at once.

The sausage produced in rural Kentucky is known as country sausage. It is a coarsely ground mixture in the usual proportion of two parts lean to one part fat. It sometimes incorporates beef with the pork. Seasoning tends to be mild compared with some of the popular foreign sausages. Part of the production is cured by adding salt to the spices and herbs used for flavoring and the sausage, stuffed into casings, is then submerged in a brine of salt, saltpeter, pepper, water and sometimes sugar. The process, very similar to that for curing country hams, retards spoilage and enhances flavor. Like country hams, many of these cured sausages are also smoked and are a delight to the palate.

Part of the country sausage production, however, is reserved for fresh sausage. It is highly perishable and cannot be kept long even under refrigeration. Nevertheless, it is delicious and easily reproduced in small batches by the home cook. It is not even necessary to encase the meat mixture since most such fresh sausage, usually called bulk sausage, is formed into patties and fried. Unlike commercial sausage, there is no question as to exactly what you put into the homemade product, in the form of preservatives or otherwise, and you can use less expensive cuts of meat (such as shoulder) and still be assured that you have wholesome ingredients. And, finally, you can custom tailor the flavorings to achieve exactly the combination that appeals to you. There is practically no limit to the scope of seasonings available. All of the following flavorings are commonly used in sausage-making and you can employ them in any combination: allspice, aniseed, basil, bay leaves, caraway seeds, cardamom, cassia, cayenne, celery seed, chili peppers, chives, cinnamon, cloves, coriander, cumin, dill, fennel, garlic, ginger, mace, marjoram, mustard, nutmeg, onions, oregano, paprika, parsley, peppercorns, sage, salt, savory and thyme. The basic bulk sausage recipe that follows can be varied to suit your taste, although I advise you not to get carried away by the endless possibilities of it all. Too many flavoring ingredients in any one dish tend to compete.

MAKING AND COOKING PORK SAUSAGE

4 pounds lean pork
2 pounds pork fat (backbone fat preferred)
2 tablespoons salt
2 tablespoons pulverized sage leaves
1 tablespoon freshly ground black pepper
¾ teaspoon red pepper
1 tablespoon dried thyme
2 teaspoons freshly grated nutmeg

Grind together the lean meat and fat, using a meat grinder or food processor. Do not overprocess. Add all of the other ingredients and knead the mixture with your hands. To test for seasoning, cook and taste a small sample. Adjust the seasoning as required. Shape the sausage into 2 loaves, wrap in waxed paper and refrigerate. When ready to use, cut into ½-inch slices or shape into patties.

Cook in a hot skillet over moderate heat, browning on both sides, about 20 minutes. Be certain the meat is thoroughly cooked before serving. Try this sausage with fried apples and corn cakes or with waffles and maple syrup.

Makes 6 pounds

Turkey With Corn Bread Stuffing And Giblet Gravy

Marcel Proust, you may recall, dipped a madeleine cookie into his tea, tasted it and was so swept away by a flood of memories that he locked himself in a cork-lined bedroom and spent years and years sitting up in bed writing volume after volume of fictionalized reminiscences. Most Americans don't have much to associate with madeleines dipped in tea, but practically everyone who got off the boat before a week ago Tuesday is subject to a flood of memories at the sight of a table laden with turkey and all the trimmings. As if one were standing in a room with mirrors on opposite walls, seeing reflections of reflections receding into space, endless echoes of Thanksgivings and Christmases past crowd in upon one: laughter, delicious smells, excitement and inevitably some sadness.

Besides being the nostalgia dish of all time, our great native food bird, the turkey, provides magnificent eating when properly prepared. Most unsuccessful roast turkeys have common failings. They are not browned properly or they are dried out; and sometimes, in my opinion, too much effort is made to enhance the bird's natural flavor and it tastes so much of sage or some other favorite herb or spice that you can't tell whether you're eating turkey or a Coney Island hot dog. The following recipe is for people who love the natural flavor of turkey and expect to find complementary and contrasting flavors in the side dishes that accompany and enhance it. The bird itself will be golden brown, juicy and bursting with natural flavor.

ROAST TURKEY

12- to 15-pound turkey
Corn Bread Stuffing (recipe follows)
¼ cup vegetable oil
Salt
Giblet Gravy (recipe follows)

Preheat the oven to 450°. Wash the turkey inside and out and pat dry. Stuff and truss the turkey. Place in a shallow roasting pan (a good size is 1½ x 12 x 21½ inches). Brush the turkey with some of the oil and sprinkle with salt. Roast the turkey for about 55 minutes, until nicely browned.

When browned, cover loosely with a sheet of aluminum foil. Continue roasting, basting at intervals, for 2 hours.

Reduce the oven heat to 375°. Continue roasting until the turkey is done, figuring on 20 to 25 minutes per pound roasting time for the stuffed bird. A thermometer inserted in the thigh should register about 185°. Or you may perform the time-honored test of pricking the thigh deeply: If the juices run clear rather than pink-tinged, the bird is done. Remove the turkey and spoon off any accumulated fat from the cooking juices. Add about ½ cup water to the roasting pan and stir to loosen and dissolve the brown particles that cling to the bottom and sides of the pan. Add this liquid to the giblet gravy. Carve the turkey and serve with the dressing and gravy.

Serves 14 to 20

CORN BREAD STUFFING

CORN BREAD:

1½ cups yellow cornmeal
1 cup all-purpose flour
1 teaspoon salt
1 tablespoon plus 1 teaspoon baking powder
2 eggs, lightly beaten
1½ cups milk
¼ cup melted bacon fat

Preheat the oven to 450°. Grease two 9-inch square pans. Sift together the cornmeal, flour, salt and baking powder in a mixing bowl. Stir in the eggs, milk and bacon fat until well mixed. Divide the batter between the baking pans. Bake for 30 minutes. Allow to cool. Crumble for making stuffing or cut into squares for corn bread.

STUFFING:

½ cup (1 stick) butter
4 medium onions, minced
Crumbled corn bread (from preceding recipe)
4 celery ribs, minced
½ teaspoon dried sage
½ teaspoon dried thyme
1 teaspoon salt
Freshly ground pepper
½ cup chicken stock

In a large skillet, melt the butter. Add the onions and sauté until soft, about 2 minutes. Stir in the crumbled corn bread. Add the celery, seasonings and stock, and mix well.

Makes enough stuffing for a 12- to 15-pound bird

GIBLET GRAVY

1 turkey neck
1 turkey gizzard
1 turkey liver
1 turkey heart, halved
Salt
3 tablespoons butter
1 tablespoon vegetable oil
Freshly ground pepper
1½ cups minced onion
3 tablespoons all-purpose flour
2½ cups chicken broth
1 bay leaf
2 parsley sprigs

Cut the neck into 1-inch lengths and set aside. Cut away the tough casing from the tender part of the gizzard. In a saucepan, combine the gizzard, liver, heart and enough cold water to cover. Add 1 teaspoon of salt and bring to a boil. Simmer for 30 minutes. Remove from the heat and drain.

Heat 2 tablespoons of the butter with the oil in a heavy saucepan. Add the neck pieces and sprinkle with salt and pepper. Cook, stirring frequently, over moderate heat for about 5 minutes, until golden brown. Add ¾ cup of the onion and cook, stirring, until the onion is translucent. Sprinkle with the flour and stir to coat evenly. Add the chicken broth, bay leaf and parsley. Bring to a boil, reduce the heat and simmer for 45 minutes.

Strain the sauce and discard the solids. Cut the giblets into fine dice.

Heat the remaining 1 tablespoon butter in a saucepan. Add the remaining ¾ cup onion and the diced giblets. Cook, stirring occasionally, over moderate heat for about 5 minutes. Add the strained sauce and bring to a boil. Simmer for about 5 minutes. Add salt and pepper to taste and serve hot.

Makes about 3 cups

VENISON ROAST

Fall is the best time for venison. In summertime, the livin' is easy for deer, too, so they are more tender and have better flavor after their annual opportunity to eat well and loaf a little. I am from that generation of Americans who absolutely refused to touch venison at first, as a result of seeing *Bambi* as a small child. But, eventually, when a friend of my father's presented us with a venison roast, my curiosity overcame my scruples. I sampled the meat and was enthralled by its flavor—familiar enough to be acceptable, yet with just a suggestion of exotic wildness.

I have enjoyed venison prepared in many different ways, so long as the cook took into account the relative dryness and toughness of the meat. Deer, after all, lead far more eventful lives than feedlot-raised steers. Thus, many of the best venison recipes are, like this one, braises that flavor and tenderize the meat by slow cooking in an aromatic liquid.

8- to 10-pound venison roast
Salt and freshly ground pepper
¼ cup (½ stick) butter
4 ounces salt pork, cut into 6 strips, ¼-inch thick
3 medium onions, minced
2 bay leaves
1 garlic clove, crushed
3 large carrots, quartered lengthwise
2½ cups vegetable stock, heated
¼ teaspoon ground allspice
¼ cup honey
2 tablespoons all-purpose flour
2 cups heavy cream
½ cup bourbon whiskey

Rub the roast thoroughly with salt and pepper.

In a large cast-iron pot or casserole, melt the butter over moderately high heat. When hot, add the roast and turn frequently until browned on all sides. Arrange the strips of salt pork over the top of the roast. Add the onions, bay leaves, garlic, carrots, hot vegetable stock, allspice, honey and additional salt and pepper. Stir the liquids thoroughly and bring the mixture to a boil. Reduce the heat to a simmer, cover and cook for 2½ hours.

Remove the roast and set aside. Strain the stock and return it to the pot. Discard the solids. Stir the flour into the heavy cream and add to the stock. Stir well and taste for seasoning. Bring to a boil. Return the roast to the gravy and simmer for 5 minutes. Stir in the bourbon and serve.

Serves 12

Pickling, Preserving and Canning

It is the way of most food crops that when they come in, they come in all at once and in quantity; and when they stop, they are finished for a whole year. Some foods, such as apples and root vegetables, can be stored fairly successfully just by keeping them dry and cool. Others, like tomatoes or peaches, can hardly be kept at all. So before the advent of year-round fresh produce imported from different climates, and before the widespread use of freezing, the only way to extend the season of most foods was to pickle, preserve or can it.

Pickling is accomplished by immersing food, whether meat, vegetable or fruit, in a saltwater brine. The amount of salt can be much reduced by adding vinegar. Over the years, of course, cooks have introduced many variations in the process. The brine can be flavored, and almost invariably is; the particular spices used determine the almost infinite variety of flavors. The pickled food can then be canned in sterilized jars, vacuum-sealed and kept indefinitely.

The preservation of fruits and vegetables, whether whole or in the form of jams, jellies, preserves and fruit butters, was accomplished in my family by a sustained and industrious frenzy of canning. The work started early in the summer with the ripening of the first berries and proceeded into the late fall when the apples and the last tomatoes were harvested. All of my relatives had kitchen gardens and some of them had farms. Anything they didn't grow was purchased in quantity from farmers who did. If your orchard grew apples, you bought peaches and pears, but not in little paper sacks. Produce was not purchased by the pound: It arrived at least by the peck and more often by the bushel.

Preserving fruits usually involves cooking them with sugar, which helps keep their color, flavor and form intact. I can just see our kitchen on a warm late summer morning with all the windows open to make the steamy activity of canning bearable. There were always at least three people working, like as not my grandmother, an aunt or two, the cook, and James Miller Williams, our handyman: Canning is a social activity. There was boiling water everywhere: one big kettle to scald the peaches in order to peel them; another to sterilize the Mason jars; a third to cook the fruit; another to seal the filled jars. There was lots of specialized equipment: canning jars with their rubber sealing rings and glass lids with wire clamps to shut out air, a giant pressure cooker with an internal rack for the final sealing of the jars, big tongs shaped for lifting canning jars out of the scalding water, skimmers and jelly testers and a pitcher of ice water to drip fruit juice into and see if it had cooked enough to gel. There were stick-on labels and a marking pen for labeling the jars in your neatest printing, and thermometers and a tripod from which was suspended a big muslin jelly bag. The jelly bag would be filled with chopped, cooked fruit until it bulged alarmingly, and a steady stream of brilliant, sweet-smelling juice poured from its bottom into a waiting kettle. As I think about it now, the clear, sweet smell of hot raspberry juice fills my head like a perfume.

Canning and preserving combine art and science. You have to know precisely what you are doing to avoid food spoilage and even, God forbid, food poisoning. There is not space here to go into the whole subject, so if you want to learn home canning, consult the government's guidelines, get a specialized book or consult one of the complete general cookbooks, such as *The Joy of Cooking* or *The Fannie Farmer Cookbook*. Several recipes for canning and preserving follow, but make sure you dot the *i*'s and cross the *t*'s by consulting an authoritative instructional guide.

BELL PEPPER CONDIMENTS

A spoonful of pepper relish or pepper jelly gives sparkle to any number of foods. Both are good with red meats, roast fowl or scrambled eggs and very welcome as a change from mayonnaise, ketchup or mustard on sandwiches. Pepper jelly recipes vary immensely: You can make a jelly from sweet red or yellow peppers, or you can make a pepper jelly that will fuse your bridgework from fiery hot chili peppers such as jalapeños. I find red pepper jellies a little insipid and chili pepper jellies too aggressive for most menus, but this green bell pepper jelly is just right. It captures the very essence of the bell pepper in its prime and is a lovely shade of green like a pale, glistening emerald. It is easy to make and provides you with raw material for the fine Red and Green Pepper Relish that follows. Since this jelly recipe requires about 5 pounds of peppers and the relish recipe calls for about 10 pounds, it is a good idea to make them when peppers are abundant and cheap.

GREEN PEPPER JELLY

5 pounds (about 12) green bell peppers, split, cored and seeded
1½ cups distilled white vinegar
7 cups sugar
2 pouches (6 ounces) Certo liquid pectin or 1 box of Sure-Jel

In a meat grinder or food processor, grind the peppers to a coarse texture; do not purée. Strain through a fine sieve to separate the juice from the pulp. (Reserve the pulp if you plan to make pepper relish.) You will need 2 cups of pepper juice. In a nonreactive saucepan, combine the juice with the vinegar and sugar. Bring to a boil and cook for 2 minutes. Add the pectin or Sure-Jel and bring back to a boil. Fill hot sterilized jars and seal properly.

Makes 6 pints

RED AND GREEN PEPPER RELISH

12 sweet green bell peppers
12 sweet red bell peppers
2 jalapeño peppers
12 medium onions
2 cups cider vinegar
2 cups cup sugar
3 tablespoons salt

In a meat grinder or food processor, grind all of the peppers and the onions to a coarse texture; do not purée. Scrape into a nonreactive saucepan and add enough water to cover (about 1 cup). Bring to a boil and boil for 5 minutes. Strain and return the solids to the saucepan. Add the vinegar, sugar and salt; boil for 5 minutes more. Fill hot, sterilized canning jars and seal properly. Will keep indefinitely.

Makes 4½ to 5 pints

CUCUMBER PICKLES

I had a cousin who, as a tiny infant, much preferred pickles to ice cream. I understand this is not uncommon, but it strikes me as strange. I don't know whether this recipe produces the kind of pickles to which she was so partial, but it is an appropriate ornament to your buffet or tailgate party. I even like them myself, though not in preference to butter pecan ice cream.

10 medium cucumbers
2 cups cider vinegar
½ cup sugar
½ teaspoon yellow mustard seed
1 teaspoon ground allspice
Coarse (kosher) salt
2 to 3 small onions, sliced

Soak the cucumbers overnight in cold water in the refrigerator. Slice crosswise ¼ inch thick. In a nonreactive saucepan, make a syrup of the vinegar, sugar, mustard seed, allspice and 1 cup water. Bring the syrup to a boil and add the cucumbers. Cook for about 3 minutes, or until the cucumbers turn pale.

Pack the pickles solidly into sterilized jars. Add 1 teaspoon of the salt and ½ sliced onion to each quart. Cover with the boiling syrup mixture and seal properly.

Makes 4 to 5 quarts

WATERMELON RIND PICKLES

These pickles are sweet and spicy with just the least amount of crunch left in them. They really are good enough to justify buying a watermelon and throwing away the center just to have the rind available for making these special pickles. And they are a special enough treat that the Barry Bingham, Srs. always served a very similar watermelon pickle at their annual Derby Breakfast along with turkey hash and paper-thin cornmeal cakes.

4 to 5 pounds peeled watermelon rinds
½ cup coarse (kosher) salt
¼ cup powdered alum
2 cups cider vinegar
2 cups sugar
2 pieces fresh ginger root (each 2 inches long), peeled and
     quartered
4 cinnamon sticks
1 tablespoon whole cloves
1 tablespoon whole allspice berries
¼ cup yellow mustard seed

Use firm, fresh watermelon rind. With a sharp knife, remove the green outer peel and all of the pink flesh from the inside surface. Cut the rind into ½-inch strips or cubes. Combine 1 gallon of water with the salt. Add the rind and soak for 24 hours.

Drain and rinse the rind. Cover with ice water and let soak for 8 hours.

Drain. Add the powdered alum to 1 gallon of water. Pour over the rind and let soak for another 12 hours.

Drain the rind and rinse well. Cover with ice water and soak for another 4 hours.

Drain, cover with fresh water and boil for 45 minutes.

In a large nonreactive pot or roaster, combine the vinegar, sugar, ginger, cinnamon, cloves, allspice and mustard seed with 1 gallon of water. Bring to a rolling boil. Add the watermelon rind and cook until the liquid is clear, about 1 hour. Divide among sterile canning jars and seal properly.

Makes 4½ pints

SWEET POTATOES WITH APPLES

This recipe is full of good Southern things—sweet potatoes, bourbon whiskey, pecans and apples. (I prefer the white variety of sweet potato.) This dish makes a very nice change from candied sweet potatoes as an accompaniment for a turkey dinner. A variation using cranberries instead of apples strikes a New England note and would be a good choice if you are not serving cranberries in some other form for your holiday dinner.

3 cups cooked, mashed sweet potatoes
2 cups cored sliced apples, preferably Winesaps
¼ cup (½ stick) butter
¼ cup granulated sugar
¼ cup packed brown sugar
½ cup finely chopped pecans
¼ cup bourbon whiskey
½ teaspoon ground cinnamon
½ teaspoon freshly grated nutmeg
½ teaspoon ground ginger

Preheat the oven to 350°. Butter a 1-quart shallow baking dish and arrange half of the mashed sweet potatoes in it. Top with the apples. Spread the remaining sweet potatoes on top. Sprinkle with half of the sugar and dot with half of the butter. Sprinkle on the pecans and bourbon. Combine the remaining sugar and butter with the spices and sprinkle over the nuts. Bake for 40 minutes, until hot and bubbly.

Variation: Substitute cranberries for the apples, use rum instead of the bourbon and increase the sugar, either white or brown, by ¼ cup.

Serves 4 to 6

MONKEY HEELS (POPCORN BALLS)

Children and popcorn balls have a natural affinity. I've found that in order to obtain popcorn balls, children will do almost anything, including shucking popcorn. We always bought ours by the bushel, on the cob. It looks about like any dried corn, and the best way to remove it from the cob is to take a popcorn cob in each hand and rub them vigorously together. This can get rather tiresome and hard on the fingers, but it keeps the younger set out of mischief and no doubt imparts a valuable moral lesson.

8 quarts popped corn
1 cup (2 sticks) butter
2 cups packed brown sugar
1 cup light corn syrup
1 teaspoon maple flavoring
1 teaspoon vanilla extract
¼ teaspoon salt
2 cups coarsely chopped pecans
½ teaspoon baking soda
Pinch of cream of tartar

Place the popcorn in a large bowl. In a saucepan, combine the butter, sugar, corn syrup, flavorings, salt and pecans. Cook for 5 minutes until well combined. Remove from the heat and stir in the baking soda and cream of tartar. Pour over the popcorn and stir to coat well. Butter your fingers and shape into 3-inch balls. Place on waxed paper. Allow to cool completely before serving.

Makes 16 to 20

GINGERBREAD MUFFINS

These muffins, which are not quite as sweet as most dessert gingerbread, are often served hot at brunch and are a huge hit with people who like sweets at breakfast, since they make an interesting change from coffee cake or sweet rolls. They also go well at luncheon with mayonnaise-based salads such as curried crab salad. And, topped with the lemon sauce recipe that follows, they can be a fine dessert.

1¾ teaspoons baking soda
1 cup buttermilk
1 cup shortening
1 cup packed light brown sugar
3 eggs
1 cup molasses
1 tablespoon powdered ginger
2 teaspoons ground cinnamon
1 teaspoon ground cloves

1 teaspoon freshly grated nutmeg
Pinch of salt
3 cups all-purpose flour, sifted

In a cup, dissolve the baking soda in the buttermilk. In a bowl, cream the shortening and sugar. Add the eggs, one at a time, beating thoroughly after each addition. Mix in the molasses. Stir the spices and salt into the flour. Add some of the flour to the creamed mixture alternately with the buttermilk until all of the ingredients are incorporated. Refrigerate the batter for at least 2 hours before baking.

Preheat the oven to 350°. Fit a muffin tin with paper cup liners. Bake for 30 to 35 minutes, or until a toothpick inserted in the center of a muffin comes out clean. If you put the muffins in to bake at the start of your meal, they will be ready, piping hot, by dessert time. Serve with the lemon sauce that follows.

Makes 12

LEMON SAUCE

2 tablespoons butter
1½ tablespoons all-purpose flour
½ cup sugar
1 cup cold water
Grated zest and juice of 1 lemon
Pinch of salt

In a small saucepan, melt the butter and stir in the flour until well combined. Add the remaining ingredients and cook, stirring, until thick.

Makes about 1 cup

GRANNY'S BLUE RIBBON APPLE PIE

This is my grandmother's recipe which may or may not have won the blue ribbon at the Taylor County Fair, but certainly won the heart and soul of anyone who ever tasted it. Grandmother was always generous with the quantity of apples she piled into the pie. The mound of apples tends to shrink during baking as the juices run down between the apple slices to mingle with the sugar and spices. She always felt that the sign of a good apple pie was the fullness and depth of its fruit (the best of which naturally came from her orchards). My mouth waters today as I dream of a slice of her pie à la mode with homemade vanilla ice cream (see recipe on page 181) or with a slice of Stilton cheese or, when it's very hot, with pure, heavy cream from the pitcher.

Unbaked 9-inch pie shell with pastry for top (page 60)
6 or 7 tart apples, peeled, cored and cut into eighths
2 tablespoons lemon or apple juice (see Note)
¾ cup granulated sugar
¼ cup packed brown sugar
1 tablespoon all-purpose flour
½ teaspoon ground cinnamon
½ teaspoon freshly grated nutmeg
Pinch of salt
3 tablespoons butter

Preheat the oven to 400°. Place the pie shell on a baking sheet. Arrange the apples in the pie shell, mounding them in the center. Sprinkle with the lemon juice. In a bowl, combine the sugars, flour, cinnamon, nutmeg and salt. Spread over the apples. Dot with the butter.

Roll out the remaining pastry. Cover the pie and crimp to form a decorative edge. With a sharp knife, cut steam vents in the top crust. Bake for 35 to 40 minutes, until browned on top.

NOTE: If you use a sweet rather than a tart apple, definitely use the lemon juice rather than the apple juice. Lemon juice also helps preserve color and flavor.

Serves 8

LONZETTA'S PUMPKIN PIE

All right, pumpkin pie with Thanksgiving dinner is a cliché. But when you invite people for Thanksgiving dinner they don't expect you to create the illusion that this is Bastille Day and you are in Paris: The more Norman Rockwell you can make the occasion the better, I say. I am grateful that my memories of Thanksgivings past include all the standard fare, and I still adhere pretty much to the classic menu, including pumpkin pie as the fitting conclusion to this legendary American feast. Serve it, sweet and spicy, with whipped cream.

½ **cup packed brown sugar**
½ **cup granulated sugar**
1½ **teaspoons ground cinnamon**
1 **teaspoon ground ginger**
½ **teaspoon salt**
½ **teaspoon freshly grated nutmeg**
½ **teaspoon ground allspice**
½ **teaspoon ground cloves**
1½ **cups cooked or canned pumpkin purée**
1 **cup heavy cream**
3 **eggs, beaten until foamy**
¼ **cup bourbon whiskey or brandy (optional)**
1 **unbaked single-crust 9-inch pie shell (page 60)**

Preheat the oven to 425°. In a bowl, combine all of the ingredients and mix well. Pour into the pie shell. Bake for 10 minutes.

Reduce the oven temperature to 325°. Bake for about 35 minutes longer or until the custard is firm.

Serves 8

PECAN BOURBON CAKE

The genius of Kentucky cooking consists, at least in part, of using what is common and available to produce something uncommon and special. As you have no doubt observed, bourbon with its unique burnished taste is much appreciated and in plentiful supply in Kentucky. Pecans, too, are cheap, plentiful and well-loved. Here they are combined in a cake for feasts of all kinds. You may already have encountered this recipe, since Mimi Sheraton included it in her splendid book of desserts, *Visions of Sugarplums.*

2 cups unsalted butter, at room temperature
2½ cups sugar
10 extra-large eggs
1 cup bourbon whiskey
2 whole nutmegs, freshly grated
3½ cups all-purpose flour
About 1 pound (15-ounce box) golden raisins
4 ounces candied citron, diced
1½ pounds shelled pecans, coarsely chopped

Preheat the oven to 250°F. Butter two 9 × 5 × 3½-inch loaf pans. Line the bottoms and sides of each with waxed paper or parchment and butter the top side of the paper. Set aside.

Cream the butter and sugar until light and fluffy. Beat the eggs lightly and gradually add to the creamed mixture, mixing well between additions. Stir in the bourbon. Add the nutmeg and flour and blend in. Stir in the raisins, citron and pecans.

Divide the batter between the prepared pans. Bake for 4 hours, or until a tester inserted into the center of the cakes comes out clean. The cakes should be moist; do not overbake.

Let the cakes cool in the pans. The completely cool cake should be wrapped in foil and stored in a cool room or refrigerated. It will taste best if allowed to ripen for 24 hours to 1 week before it is cut. For a more pronounced bourbon flavor, soak a length of new cheesecloth in the whiskey, then wrap the wrung-out cloth around the cake. Wrap in foil and store in a cool place. Pull back only as much paper as needed to cut the slices you want for each serving. This keeps in the freezer or refrigerator for months. It is best cut into slices of just a little less than ½ inch thick.

Variation: A half-and-half combination of pecans and black walnuts may be used.
Makes 2 loaf cakes

SHAKER LEMON PIE

This shaker recipe is unusual in that the pie is filled with sliced whole lemons, including the rind. You would expect such a pie to be overpowered by the bitter oils in the rind, but you can trust the Shakers about food—they are always right. The period during which the lemons stand in sugar seems to draw their juices and neutralize the bitter oils. The resulting pie has a delightful, slightly chewy texture imparted by the rind, and is a welcome change from the usual lemon chiffon or lemon meringue pie.

2 large lemons
2 cups sugar
4 eggs, well beaten
1 unbaked 9-inch pie shell with pastry for a top (page 60)

In a bowl, slice the lemons paper-thin, rind and all. Pick out the seeds. Combine with the sugar and mix well. Let stand 2 hours or longer, stirring occasionally.

Preheat the oven to 450°. Add the beaten eggs to the lemon mixture and mix well. Pour into the pie shell, arranging the lemon slices evenly. Roll out the remaining pastry and cover the pie. Cut several slits near the center. Bake for 15 minutes. Reduce the heat to 375°. Bake for about 20 minutes more, or until the top of a knife inserted in the center comes out clean. Cool before serving.

Serves 8

CHESS PIE

When I was a little boy I remember asking Anna Smith, our cook at that time, why my favorite pie was called chess pie. She said, "Why, Honey, that's 'cause it so good that every young lady needs a receipt for it in her hope chess." She was a wonderful woman and one of the best cooks in Campbellsville, but not above making things up to please a little boy. I've never had a lot of faith in her as an etymologist. A more likely theory is that the dish was originally called "lemon cheese" by the English, who originated it. The phrase was apparently corrupted by the early settlers of Virginia, which in those days included Kentucky. In any event, this pie, if properly made, has a lightly caramelized, slightly chewy top with a light-colored, delicious custard under it. There's a favorite Southern recipe for a rich, sugary pie called Jefferson Davis Pie, page 169, which closely resembles it. There are many variations on the basic sugar pie, several of which appear in this book, but in one form or another it has survived for generations as a perennial favorite.

½ cup (1 stick) butter, at room temperature
1¾ cups sugar
3 egg yolks
2 whole eggs
1 cup heavy cream
2 teaspoons ground cinnamon
2 teaspoons freshly grated nutmeg
1 unbaked single-crust 9-inch pie shell (page 60)

Preheat the oven to 450°. Cream together the butter and sugar. Add the egg yolks and whole eggs separately, beating thoroughly after each addition until mixture is lemony in color. Add the cream and spices.

Pour into the pie shell. Bake for 15 minutes. Reduce the heat to 350°. Bake for 30 to 40 minutes longer, or until a brown crusty top forms and a toothpick inserted in the center comes out clean.

Serves 8

CREAMY PRALINES

This pecan candy is an old Southern favorite that has become popular all over the country. I suspect that in the North it is more familiar chopped up in vanilla ice cream than served in a candy dish, but it is wonderful either way. This recipe, because of the added half-and-half, is not as brittle and crunchy as most pralines, having, as the name suggests, a creamy texture.

2 cups granulated sugar
1 cup packed brown sugar
¼ cup (½ stick) unsalted butter
½ cup half-and-half
¼ teaspoon salt
3 cups coarsely chopped pecans

Combine all the ingredients except the pecans in a heavy saucepan. Bring to a rolling boil. Add the pecans. Continue cooking until the mixture reaches the soft ball stage, 234° to 238° on a candy thermometer. Remove from the heat. Stir vigorously until the candy looks creamy and begins to stiffen. Spoon out into 1½ to 2-inch rounds on waxed paper and cool to room temperature.

Makes about 1½ pounds

KENTUCKY TOMBSTONE PUDDING

The name of this three-layered dessert is a little farfetched, perhaps the fancy of a cook who sampled the sherry that flavors it a little too enthusiastically, but you'll find the inspiration for the name in the recipe itself. I don't really see how you could make a pudding resemble a tombstone very closely unless you were to spell out "R.I.P." in maraschino cherries on the top, but the name is certainly shorter than "Sherry-Macaroon-Almond-Meringue Delight Pudding,"although that sums it up. Besides, kids love sinister nomenclature. The alcohol cooks out, so you can serve this dessert at Halloween.

6 egg yolks
1 cup plus 2 tablespoons sugar
1 teaspoon all-purpose flour
1 cup sweet sherry
2 dozen almond macaroons
3 egg whites
Pinch of salt
Pinch of cream of tartar
½ cup whole blanched almonds

Preheat the oven to 300°. In a double-boiler, whisk the egg yolks until thick and lemon-colored. Combine 1 cup of the sugar and the flour; whisk into the yolks. Add the sherry and place over simmering water. Cook, stirring constantly, until thick enough to coat the back of a spoon.

Arrange the macaroons in a 2-quart shallow ovenproof baking dish. Pour the custard over them. Place the egg whites in a large bowl. Add the salt and cream of tartar and beat until stiff, gradually adding the remaining 2 tablespoons of sugar. Spread the meringue over the custard to cover completely. Stud with the almonds (tombstones!, you see?) and bake for about 15 minutes, or until lightly browned. Serve hot.

Serves 8

Kentucky Inns

$\mathcal{E}$xploring the beautiful and varied terrain of the state of Kentucky is one of the finest things I know to do. There are mist-covered mountains, part of the Appalachian range, in the East. The celebrated Bluegrass country, in north central Kentucky, is like a great rolling lawn studded with immense shade trees and bounded by the characteristic white fences of Kentucky's foremost breeding farms and racing stables. South of the Bluegrass is the Knob country, named for the odd, rounded rock formations and brooding escarpment that rise above its fields and forests. The escarpment marks the Knob country's southernmost boundary, while below it are the gently rolling farmlands and steep forest-covered hills of the Pennyrile, whose name derives from the region's abundant pennyroyal, a plant related to wild mint. To the west, the elevation drops off sharply to the wide flood plain dotted with man-made lakes and wild bird marshes, notable for fishing and hunting as well as water sports. Stretching to Kentucky's western boundary along the mighty Mississippi River, the plain forms part of the great central flyway along which millions of ducks and geese migrate twice each year.

In addition to its natural beauty, Kentucky is fortunate in still possessing a number of historic places of public dining and accommodation, in which the traditions of its cooking and hospitality continue virtually unbroken from the very early days of the Republic. It is an oddity of our history that there should be 200 year old inns still operating in Kentucky, which at the time of the Revolution was untamed wilderness largely covered by virgin forest. Vast herds of buffalo then roamed the Bluegrass, and the early white settlers were often caught in Indian forays. Nevertheless, during this time the Talbott Tavern, the oldest existing western stagecoach stop in the nation and the first permanent building in Bardstown, was constructed as a public house, and is still serving travelers traditional food of the kind represented by its recipes in the following pages. The Old Stone Inn in Harrodsburg was originally built as a private house (although a highly fortified one, in view of the dangers of the time) in about 1792, and within a year or two of its completion had been converted to the hostelry that still provides excellent food and service today.

Civilization came rapidly to Kentucky during the early days of the Republic. The Moore house in Bowling Green (now Mariah's 1818) is no potential fortress but rather a refined town house of its time. By 1825 a school for young ladies was operating at Science Hill in a building begun in the early 1790s. Another school to educate the daughters of the increasingly prosperous Kentuckians opened at Harrodsburg in 1845. These two early beacons of civilization are now inns—Science Hill Inn and Beaumont Inn. Lest you get the impression that all the educational institutions in the state have given up their missions to supply room and board consider Boone Tavern, the hospitality center of an admirable school of higher education, Berea College, which has taken to itself the task of educating the sons and daughters of Appalachia. A hundred years before Boone Tavern was founded the intrepid Shakers had settled on their lovely acreage called Pleasant Hill and were building the largest intact Shaker community in the United States and living in their own odd but affecting way.

More recent additions to the list include a beautiful antebellum Southern plantation house, which in fact didn't assume that appearance until the 1920s when a structure built in 1873 was handsomely redesigned in a tribute to an earlier tradition and became The Mansion at Griffin Gate.

By the beginning of the twentieth century the awesome wilderness of the 1700s was long tamed, and Louisville had become a major city requiring luxurious modern facilities for visitors and public rooms suitable for the social requirements of the polished and wealthy residents of the city. This led to the construction of The Seelbach Hotel in 1905 and The Brown in 1923. Kentucky lost The Brown for a time and was in danger of losing The Seelbach, as you will see, but those stories have a happy ending. In fact, some of the adversities of the past have served Kentucky well. From the beginning of the Great Depression of the 1930s through World War II virtually nothing was built in Kentucky, and the post-war prosperity touched the state very lightly. Kentuckians therefore didn't bulldoze their past to construct characterless modern buildings, with the result that they still have a considerable heritage of buildings well worth preserving. Many of the landmark inns that welcomed travelers from as long ago as the beginnings of our Republic are still in operation, and still providing accommodations and cooking that evoke the best of the past.

Beaumont Inn, Harrodsburg

I remember being taken to lunch at the Beaumont Inn for the first time many years ago by my father. It was a lovely spring day in April and we were on our way to look in on the races at Keeneland. The Bluegrass countryside was carpeted with the fresh green of spring, and we saw everywhere the blossoming dogwoods, redbud and azaleas. The inn itself, a graceful Greek Revival structure of old soft-pink brick with a white-columned portico and windows framed with black shutters, is surrounded by extensive grounds filled with flowering plants and towering old hardwood maple trees. The door, opened by a white-coated butler, leads into an antiques-filled interior of cool high-ceilinged rooms; I half expected to meet Scarlett O'Hara hurrying around the next corner. In fact the building was constructed as a fashionable girls' school in 1845 and subsequently became known first as Daughters College and then as Beaumont College. Then 70 years ago Annie Belle Goddard, a dean in the college, bought the place and converted it into an inn with a dining room. Her descendants, the Dedman family, now in the fourth generation, are still operating the inn and serving many of Kentucky's best-loved specialties.

Beaumont Inn has long been noted for its country ham, but you already have a good recipe for that. Here instead are some other recipes from the Dedmans' book, *Beaumont Inn Special Recipes*. One that they particularly wanted me to use is Corn Pudding, which is on the menu for luncheon and dinner every day the inn is open. The second is a Huguenot Torte which I'm very grateful to have; my family is partly Huguenot (early French Protestant), and I've never been able to track down the recipe for a similar cake that I used to love as a child.

CORN PUDDING

**2 cups fresh or frozen whole corn kernels (if frozen, corn must
    be thawed and drained)**
½ cup all-purpose flour
1 teaspoon salt
1½ tablespoons sugar
¼ cup (½ stick) butter, melted
4 eggs, beaten
4 cups milk

Preheat the oven to 325°. In a bowl, combine the corn, flour, salt, sugar and melted butter. Beat the eggs with the milk. Combine both mixtures and stir. Pour into a shallow baking pan or baking dish. Bake for 40 to 45 minutes, stirring 3 times during the baking, until set.

Serves 4 to 6

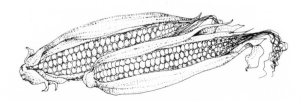

HUGUENOT TORTE

This recipe was also a favorite of my aunt-by-marriage, Mabel Newton Felts, a devoted Huguenot and president of her patriotic organization.

3 eggs
2 cups sugar
⅓ cup all-purpose flour
1 tablespoon plus ½ teaspoon baking powder
¼ teaspoon salt
1½ teaspoons vanilla extract
1½ cups chopped apples
1½ cups coarsely chopped pecans
Whipped cream and maraschino cherries for serving

Preheat the oven to 350°. Heavily butter an oblong glass baking dish. Beat the eggs and sugar with an electric mixer until light. Sift together the flour, baking powder and salt. Add to the egg and sugar mixture and mix at low speed or by hand. Stir in the vanilla, apples and nuts. Spread in an even layer in the prepared pan, spreading part of the batter up the sides of the pan.

Bake for 30 to 40 minutes, or until the torte puffs up and then falls again and is pale brown in color. Do not overcook; the torte burns easily.

While still hot, scrape down the sides of the pan. Cool on a rack. Cut into 16 squares. Serve with whipped cream and top with a cherry.

Serves 16

Science Hill Inn, Shelbyville

Science Hill Inn, like the Beaumont Inn, began as a girls' school, and an even longer time ago. Part of the building complex on Science Hill dates from the early 1790s and the school opened there in 1825. The school kept expanding and rather than build new structures they just kept adding on to the old. The result is a wonderfully rambling but harmonious structure which today houses a variety of exclusive shops as well as the Wakefield-Searce Galleries, carrying a spectacular array of antique furniture and silver. Beautiful silver in the form of tea services and julep cups, created by such famous Kentucky silversmiths as Paul Storr, has long been treasured in Kentucky, and may be found in many private homes as well as in fine shops.

The Georgian Room, the dining room at Science Hill, is decorated in the style of the early 1800s. It features beautifully prepared dishes such as these recipes graciously provided for use in this book by Donna and Terry Gill, hosts of the Science Hill Inn and featured in the book *Donna Gill Recommends.*

PORK TENDERLOIN WITH MUSTARD SAUCE

12 slices pork tenderloin, cut ¾ inch thick
Salt and freshly ground pepper
All-purpose flour
5 tablespoons butter
⅓ cup white wine vinegar
8 black peppercorns, crushed
2 cups heavy cream
½ cup Dijon mustard

Place each slice of pork tenderloin between 2 sheets of waxed paper and pound until flattened to ½ inch thick. Sprinkle with salt and pepper and dust with flour. In a skillet, melt 3 tablespoons of the butter. Sauté the pork on both sides until just done. Transfer to a platter and keep warm.

Add the vinegar and crushed peppercorns to the skillet. Bring to a boil and deglaze the pan, scraping up the browned bits that cling to the bottom of the pan, and boiling until the liquid is reduced by two-thirds. Add the heavy cream and simmer until thickened. Remove from the heat and stir in the mustard and the remaining 2 tablespoons butter. Season to taste and pour over the pork.

Serves 6

AUTUMN DUCK

1 tablespoon butter
1 tablespoon oil
4- to 5-pound duck, cut up
2 large red onions
2 tablespoons sugar
½ teaspoon dried thyme
¼ teaspoon ground coriander
¼ teaspoon ground ginger
1 parsley sprig
Salt and freshly ground pepper
2 cups beef stock
3 cups (2 cans) beer
1 box (11 ounces) mixed dried fruit
2 tablespoons all-purpose flour
Chopped parsley (optional)

Preheat the oven to 325°. In a heavy skillet, melt the butter with the oil. Dry off the duck pieces and brown slowly to render the duck fat. Place the duck pieces in an enameled casserole dish as they are browned.

Remove all but ¼ cup fat from the browning skillet. Add the sliced onions and sauté until limp and golden. Sprinkle with the sugar and add to the casserole. Add the remaining seasonings and parsley to the casserole, along with the beef stock and beer.

Cover the casserole and bake for 1½ hours. Add the dried fruit, cover and bake for another 30 minutes.

Remove the duck and fruit to a serving dish and keep warm. Degrease the cooking juices and thicken the sauce with the flour. Season to taste with salt and pepper and pour over the duck. Garnish with chopped parsley, if desired, and serve.

Serves 4

BISCUIT PUDDING WITH BOURBON SAUCE

If this cookbook starts you making biscuits regularly, you'll often have some leftover ones on hand, a wonderful excuse for serving this tasty pudding with bourbon sauce. The recipe is particularly good if you use the Cream of Tartar Biscuits on page 57.

10 buttered biscuits (1½ inches in diameter)
4 cups milk
6 eggs
2 cups sugar
2 tablespoons vanilla extract
¼ cup melted butter

Preheat the oven to 350°. Break the biscuits into small pieces and place in a large bowl. Add the milk and set aside to soak for 30 minutes.

Beat the eggs with the sugar and vanilla and add to the biscuit mixture. Pour the melted butter into a 2-quart baking dish. Add the pudding. Bake for 1 hour, until set. Serve warm with Bourbon Sauce.

Serves 4 to 6

BOURBON SAUCE

½ cup (1 stick) butter
1 cup sugar
1 egg
⅓ cup bourbon whiskey

In a heavy saucepan, melt the butter. Add the sugar and ¼ cup water and cook over moderate heat, stirring occasionally, for 5 minutes. In a separate bowl, beat the egg. Remove the butter mixture from the heat. Gradually add to the egg, whisking constantly. Stir in the bourbon and serve.

Makes about 1½ cups

Louisville's Grand Hotels:
The Seelbach And The Brown

Louisville is fortunate enough to have two grand hotels—The Seelbach and The Brown. The Seelbach Hotel opened in 1905 during the Belle Epoque and instantly became indispensable to Louisville social life. It was a resplendent big-city hotel in the Beaux Arts style, filled top to bottom with elegant appointments. The lobby walls were covered with murals of the history of Kentucky and the Northwest Territory. An arched ceiling of glass skylights soared high above the lobby on columns of marble, and the grand staircase and lobby floor were of marble, too. The main dining room was paneled in fine oak wainscoting and the vaulted ceramic arches of the subterranean Rathskeller were made by the famous Rookwood Pottery Company. In short, no expense was spared, and the investment paid off in the form of a national reputation for Louisville's proud new hostelry. The Seelbach had the market to itself until 1923, when a brash entrepreneur named James Graham Brown decided that there was demand enough for another fine hotel in Louisville. He built an even larger hotel just down the street and named it after himself.

The opening of The Brown Hotel in 1923 made Louisville practically giddy with excitement. Fifteen stories high and incorporating 600 rooms, it was described as the largest modern hotel south of Chicago. No expense was spared to make The Brown opulent. There were high, coffered ceilings finely detailed in gilt and carved stone with cast plaster moldings, ornamented arcades and elaborate furnishings. Food and drink were available in the Thoroughbred Room, the English Grill and the Bluegrass Room, while banquets were served in the Crystal Ballroom. The food was wonderful. I remember going into Louisville for Christmas shopping during my college days and always having at least one of The Brown's superb hard rolls while waiting for that perennial luncheon favorite called, rather eccentrically, "The Hot Brown."

The Brown became the premier gathering place during the 1920s, but The Seelbach kept a loyal following, and it was generally agreed that Louisville was big enough for two first-class hotels. Indeed, at Derby time Louisville could fill 20 first-class hotels.

The crash of 1929 and the subsequent Depression put the finances of both hotels under some strain, but against heavy odds they continued their tradition of fine service throughout and even during World War II. During the post-war period, however, changes began to be felt. Downtown Louisville began a slow decline, and that unsatisfactory American institution, the motel, began to siphon off much of the hotels' business.

The Seelbach slowly lost its grandeur through lack of maintenance and ill-considered attempts at renewal. The lobby murals were covered over and a dropped ceiling concealed the arching skylights.

As for The Brown, it was closed entirely after the death of James Graham Brown, and in 1971 became the headquarters of the Louisville Department of Education.

Then in recent years a sort of miracle happened. The leaders of the city decided that downtown Louisville could be saved by reviving those symbols of elegance, the grand hotels. The Seelbach was restored to its former beauty with a great deal of love and money. The Brown, purchased from the city by the Hilton hotel chain, was made more elegant than ever: the number of rooms was halved and their size doubled, and all the original detail in the hotel was restored. Both hotels put a great deal of emphasis and effort into providing the kind of food that had made them famous. The Brown had to research the recipe for The Hot Brown, graciously given us for reproduction here, since the original formula had been lost. The other recipe from The Brown, Chicken Chow Mein, although it may seem a little odd in a book devoted to Kentucky cooking, was for many years prior to the closing of The Brown one of the most popular dishes on the menu. I doubt if anything like it has ever been served in China, whereas oceans of it have been served in Louisville, so in my book this has to be regarded as Kentucky food.

THE HOT BROWN

6 tablespoons butter
½ cup plus 2 tablespoons all-purpose flour
1½ cups half-and-half
1½ cups heavy cream
⅓ cup grated romano cheese
⅓ cup grated Parmesan cheese
½ cup sweet sherry, boiled for 1 minute
2 egg yolks, beaten
4 toast points
½ pound turkey breast slices
4 tomato wedges
4 strips crisp cooked bacon
Parsley

In a heavy saucepan, melt the butter. Sprinkle on the flour and stir constantly until the roux is golden and dry.

Stir in the half-and-half and the cream. Cook several minutes, or until the flour taste is gone. Stir in the romano and Parmesan cheeses. Add the sherry and continue stirring until the sauce is thin and the cheese is melted.

Strain the hot sauce into a bowl. Add the egg yolks and blend well. The sauce may be reheated, but do not boil.

Preheat the broiler. Line 2 ovenproof single serving dishes with 2 toast points. Top with slices of turkey and a generous covering of sauce. Broil until the sauce is lightly browned on top.

Remove and place 2 tomato wedges and 2 bacon strips criss-crossed, on each sandwich. Garnish with parsley. Serve hot.

Serves 2

BROWN HOTEL CHICKEN CHOW MEIN

3-pound spring chicken
Celery, onion and carrots for broth
1 celery rib, cut into fine julienne, 1½ inches long
3 medium onions, thinly sliced
3 cups mushrooms, cleaned and sliced
4 tablespoons (½ stick) butter
1 can (8 ounces) bean sprouts, drained
1 can (8 ounces) water chestnuts, drained and sliced
½ cup plus 2 tablespoons bead molasses (Chinese soy) (see Note)
Soy sauce
2 tablespoons cornstarch
Fried Chinese noodles, 1 quartered hard-cooked egg per serving,
**   leek julienne and cashews, for garnishes**

Cover the chicken generously with water. Add the celery, onions and carrots to flavor the broth. Simmer until the chicken stock is well done. *Save the stock.*

In a skillet, melt the butter over moderate heat. Add the celery, onions and mushrooms and sauté until just limp.

When the chicken is done discard the skin and bones. Julienne the chicken meat. Strain the stock and return the julienned chicken to the stock and add the sautéed vegetables. Add the bean sprouts and sliced water chestnuts. Add the bead molasses and soy sauce and bring the chow mein to a boil for about 5 minutes.

Mix the cornstarch with 2 tablespoons cold water. Add to the chow mein and stir to thicken slightly.

To serve, put fried Chinese noodles on a plate and cover with chow mein. Sprinkle with more noodles. Garnish each end of the plate with 2 hard-cooked egg quarters. Sprinkle the leeks julienne and cashews on top.

NOTE: Bead or Chinese soy molasses can be found in Oriental specialty food shops.

Serves 6 to 8

SEELBACH HOTEL VEAL SCALLOPINI

4 pieces veal loin (2½ ounces each)
All-purpose flour
2 tablespoons unsalted butter
1 tablespoon vegetable oil
8 to 10 button mushrooms, sliced
2 shallots, diced
½ cup finely chopped fresh basil
1 cup dry white wine
2 tablespoons all-purpose flour
½ cup heavy cream
2 teaspoons Pommery mustard
Salt and freshly ground white pepper
¼ cup toasted pine nuts
2 cups cooked pasta, ribbon or bow-tie shaped

One slice at a time, pound the veal between 2 sheets of waxed paper until flat. Dust lightly with flour. In a skillet, heat ½ tablespoon of the butter and 1 tablespoon vegetable oil. Sauté the veal and place on a warm serving platter.

Add ½ tablespoon butter, the mushrooms and diced shallots to the sauté pan and sauté briefly over high heat. Add the basil. Add the white wine and reduce by half. Add the flour and brown. Next add the heavy cream. Add the mustard and remaining butter. Season to taste.

Arrange the veal over the warm pasta and top with the sauce. Garnish with toasted pine nuts.

Serves 2

SEELBACH HOTEL GRILLED SALMON WITH HERBS

2½ pounds Pacific salmon steaks
1 teaspoon fresh chopped basil
1 teaspoon fresh chopped thyme
1 teaspoon fresh chopped parsley
½ clove garlic, peeled and minced
1½ cups olive oil
2 teaspoons fresh lemon juice
2 teaspoons fresh lime juice
2 teaspoons fresh orange juice
¼ cup (½ stick) butter, softened
Additional slices of lemon, lime and orange
½ teaspoon white pepper
½ teaspoon salt

Arrange the salmon steaks in a shallow glass dish. Combine the basil, thyme, parsley and garlic in the olive oil. Marinate the salmon in the herb/oil mixture for 24 hours.

Add the lemon, lime and orange juices to the butter and mix thoroughly to make citrus butter.

Grill the salmon over high heat for 3 minutes per side or until desired doneness, grilling the fleshy side of the salmon first. Spread the citrus butter on the salmon, season with pepper and salt and garnish with the sliced fruit.

Serves 8 to 10

Old Stone Inn, Simpsonville

In about 1792 massive amounts of stone were loaded into ox carts two counties away and laboriously hauled to Simpsonville for the construction of Fleming P. Rogers' house. Shelby County had been only recently wrested from the Indians with difficulty, having been the site of many a bloody massacre and skirmish. Thus the walls of Mr. Rogers' house were solid stone and almost 2 feet thick. The floors were of ship oak, each of the 11 rooms had its own fireplace, and the best materials and workmanship were used throughout, with the unfortunate result that by the time the building was completed in about 1794 Rogers had become overextended and had to sell his house without ever living in it. It became a stagecoach stop for travelers in Kentucky, and has been providing public hospitality ever since as the Old Stone Inn. After almost 200 years the original floors are still intact, and the house—now a restaurant noted for its excellent food—is furnished throughout with handsome antique furniture. One of my aunts used to give a pre-Derby dinner party at the Old Stone Inn, and I can still remember the dazzling white tablecloths on the tables and the white formal mess jackets worn by the staff.

Today there is very little danger of Indian attack, but the area provides a happier if more tranquil excitement. Simpsonville is situated between Louisville and Lexington in the middle of the Bluegrass horse-breeding country, and many of the beautiful and well-known farms can be visited.

SCALLOPED ZUCCHINI

4 large zucchini, cut into ½-inch rounds
4 hard-cooked eggs, chopped
1 cup heavy cream
1½ cups grated sharp cheddar cheese
1 teaspoon Tabasco sauce
1 teaspoon Worcestershire sauce
½ cup bread crumbs

Preheat the oven to 350°. Butter an 8-inch square baking dish. Layer the zucchini and eggs alternately in the pan, ending with a layer of eggs. Mix together the cream, 1 cup cheddar cheese, Tabasco sauce and Worcestershire sauce. Pour the mixture evenly over the casserole. Sprinkle the top with the remaining cheese and bread crumbs. Bake for 40 to 45 minutes, or until the zucchini is easily pierced with a fork and the top of the casserole is lightly browned.

Serves 6

STUFFED EGGPLANT

1 large eggplant
½ teaspoon salt
¼ cup chopped onion
½ cup sliced mushrooms
1 tablespoon butter
1 cup heavy cream
1 teaspoon Worcestershire sauce
1 cup fine butter-type cracker crumbs (about 24)
1 tablespoon chopped parsley

Preheat the oven to 375°. Slice the eggplant in half lengthwise. Remove the pulp to within ½ inch of skin. Dice the removed pulp and place in a saucepan. Add ½ cup water and the salt. Simmer until the eggplant is tender. Drain. Sauté the onion and mushrooms in the butter until golden brown. Stir the onion, mushrooms, cream, Worcestershire sauce and all but 2 tablespoons of the cracker crumbs into the eggplant pulp. Fill the eggplant shells with the mixture. Place the eggplant halves in a shallow baking pan. Sprinkle the top with the reserved crumbs and parsley. Pour water into the baking pan around the eggplant halves. Bake for 1 hour or until piping hot.

Serves 4

Old Talbott Tavern, Bardstown

Bardstown, which many Kentuckians pronounce "barge-town," is one of the prettiest towns in Kentucky or anyplace else. It is filled with lovely old houses from the early 1800s in the Greek Revival or Georgian Colonial styles. They are built of handmade bricks in soft, weathered pink or painted dazzling white, and they stand along broad streets bordered by huge, stately old shade trees. In the center of town stands St. Joseph's Proto-Cathedral, built of local limestone and brick, its classic portico supported by Ionic columns carved from huge poplar trees felled in the forest that once adjoined the town. ("Proto-cathedral," in case you're wondering, means that this church was the first Roman Catholic cathedral in Kentucky, but the bishop subsequently moved his seat to Louisville.) Inside the church is a very impressive collection of paintings. They are said to have been a gift from Louis Philippe, but more likely they were bought by the local bishop from looted churches in Belgium and France during the Napoleonic wars. Bardstown is a Catholic island in a sea of Baptists.

I used to love to drive guests to Bardstown for the sound-and-light show of My Old Kentucky Home featuring the music of Stephen Collins Foster and historical costumes. We always had dinner beforehand at the Old Talbott Tavern, which stands on Courthouse Square. Indeed, it has stood there longer than the square, since it was the first permanent building here and was constructed to be a public house, which it still is. It has provided food, drink and lodging for the night to travelers for over two centuries, ever since it was licensed by Virginia's Governor Patrick Henry. It is the oldest western stagecoach stop in America, and during its long history has played host to a wonderfully varied assortment of notable people, among them Louis Philippe, king of France; Jesse James, outlaw; Abraham Lincoln, then a child; John J. Audubon, naturalist; George Rogers Clark, explorer; Stephen Foster, composer; John Fitch, steamboat inventor; Daniel Boone, mountain man; and George S. Patton, fighting man. It's rather a shame they all couldn't have gathered at the tavern at the same time to enjoy both conversation and the excellent traditional Kentucky specialties. At the very least I imagine that the king would have asked Jesse James just why he shot bullets into the murals that one of the king's party had painted on the walls of the second floor dining room. You can still see both the murals and the bullet holes. At any rate, here are a few dishes they all might have enjoyed.

CRANBERRY BREAD

2 cups sifted all-purpose flour
1 cup sugar
1½ teaspoons baking powder
1 teaspoon salt
½ teaspoon baking soda
¼ cup (½ stick) butter
1 egg, beaten
1 teaspoon grated orange zest
¾ cup fresh orange juice
1½ cups raisins
1½ cups chopped fresh or frozen cranberries

Preheat the oven to 350°. Butter a standard loaf pan. Sift the flour, sugar, baking powder, salt and baking soda into a large bowl. Cut in the butter until the mixture is crumbly. Add the egg, orange zest and orange juice all at once. Stir just until the mixture is evenly moistened. Fold in the raisins and cranberries.

Spoon into the loaf pan. Bake for 1 hour and 10 minutes or until a toothpick inserted in the center comes out clean. After cooling for 5 to 10 minutes in the pan, remove from the pan and cool on a rack.

Makes 1 loaf

CORN FRITTERS

3 cups all-purpose flour
1½ teaspoons baking powder
½ teaspoon salt
1 cup whole corn kernels
1 egg
Pinch of sugar
¼ cup milk
Vegetable oil, for deep frying
½ cup confectioners' sugar, for serving

In a bowl, combine the flour, baking powder and salt. Add the corn, egg and sugar. Stir in the milk to form a dough that is soft but not runny.

In a deep-fryer heat the oil to 325°. Drop rounded tablespoons of fritter dough into the oil and fry for about 10 to 15 minutes, or until golden brown. Drain on paper towels for about 2 minutes. Roll in powdered sugar. Serve warm.

Serves 6 to 8

JAM CAKE WITH CARAMEL ICING

CAKE

1 cup (2 sticks) butter, at room temperature
1½ cups sugar
3 eggs
2 cups all-purpose flour
½ teaspoon salt
2 teaspoons ground cinnamon
1 teaspoon freshly grated nutmeg
1 teaspoon baking soda
1 cup buttermilk
1 cup blackberry jam
1 cup chopped pecans
⅔ cup seedless raisins

Preheat the oven to 350°. Butter and flour two 9-inch cake pans. In a bowl, cream the butter. Add the sugar and cream again. Add the eggs 1 at a time, beating well after each addition. Sift together the flour, salt and spices; stir into the creamed mixture. Dissolve the soda in the buttermilk. Add half of the buttermilk and mix. Add the remaining buttermilk and mix again. Fold in the jam, nuts and raisins; mix well. Divide between the cake pans. Bake for 40 minutes, or until a toothpick inserted in the center comes out clean. Remove from oven and let the layers cool for 5 to 10 minutes. Run a knife around the edges of the pans to loosen and invert the layers onto a rack to cool completely.

ICING:

2¼ cups packed light brown sugar
1 cup heavy cream
2 tablespoons light corn syrup
⅓ cup butter
½ teaspoon vanilla extract

In a heavy saucepan, combine the sugar, cream and corn syrup. Cook to the soft ball stage, 234° to 238°, or until the mixture forms a soft ball when dropped into a glass of ice water. Remove from the heat. Add the butter and vanilla and beat until creamy.

Serves about 12

The Mansion At Griffin Gate, Lexington

The capitol of the Bluegrass region is Lexington. Sitting in New York, it is hard to imagine in this day and age that the breeding, raising and training of thoroughbred race horses is a major industry, and yet in Lexington it seems the most natural thing in the world. For miles in all directions the lush rolling meadows are bisected by the white-painted horse fences of great breeding farms and world-famous racing stables. Racehorse enthusiasts from everywhere converge on Lexington annually for the auctions of yearlings and the races at Keeneland track. The Queen of England attends most years, not as head of state but as a lover of fine horses and the owner of a great racing stable.

Photographs of thoroughbred mares and their foals browsing under the trees in a Bluegrass pasture in springtime are the very symbol of Kentucky to many people. There is a restaurant on the outskirts of Lexington which is also a picture-perfect representation of the horse country, the Mansion at Griffin Gate. Actually, the house is comparatively new by the standards of some of the Kentucky inns in this chapter, having been built only a hundred or so years ago in 1873. It only assumed its present appearance in the 1920s, but it is a beauty.

The menu, too, is less traditionally Kentuckian than some of the others, providing a fine change from its patrons' customary fare, but the dishes are imaginative and beautifully prepared.

ASPARAGUS WITH RASPBERRY HOLLANDAISE

2 pounds cooked asparagus spears (for cooking instructions, see page 33)

HOLLANDAISE SAUCE:

3 egg yolks
3 tablespoons lemon juice
½ teaspoon salt
⅛ teaspoon cayenne pepper
¾ cup (1½ sticks) butter

Combine all of the ingredients except the butter in a blender. Mix thoroughly. Heat the butter until almost bubbling. Gradually add the butter to the egg mixture while the blender is running. Mix for an additional 1 minute.

RASPBERRY SAUCE:

**1 pint fresh raspberries
1½ cups white wine
½ cup sugar**

In a small, heavy saucepan, combine the raspberries, wine and sugar. Bring to a boil and then reduce the heat to low. Simmer for 30 minutes. Strain through a fine sieve and set aside to cool. Reserve ½ cup for the Raspberry Hollandaise. Store the rest in the refrigerator.

Arrange the asparagus on a serving platter. Warm the hollandaise sauce in the top part of a double boiler and add ½ cup raspberry sauce. Blend well and pour over the asparagus.

Serves 8

SICILIAN POTATO CASSEROLE

**¾ cup pepperoni, sliced
4 baking potatoes, peeled and thinly sliced
1 teaspoon minced garlic
½ red bell pepper, chopped
½ green bell pepper, chopped
¼ cup black olives, chopped
½ cup grated Parmesan cheese
Salt and freshly ground pepper
1 cup heavy cream**

Line the bottom of a 1 quart casserole with sliced pepperoni. Add a layer of sliced potatoes, garlic, red and green peppers, black olives, Parmesan cheese and salt and pepper to taste. Top with another layer and continue adding layers until all ingredients are used. Pour in the heavy cream. Seal the top tightly with aluminum foil and bake in 350° oven for 45 minutes to 1 hour, until bubbly and golden brown.

Serves 6

Mariah's 1818 Restaurant, Bowling Green

Bowling Green sits on high ground above the Barren River in south central Kentucky, an area of many lakes surrounded by state parklands and of a national park boasting the world's longest cave system. Bowling Green got its rather peculiar name from the form of recreation employed by the town's first judicial personnel. Robert and George Moore, the Virginians who founded Bowling Green, used to hold sessions of the county court in Robert's house. During court recesses the lawyers, judges and clerks, and I suppose the plaintiffs, defendants and witnesses used to pass the time by playing bowls in the front yard. No doubt it lent a cordial tone to the judicial proceedings. In any event, for some reason the name stuck and the whole town became known as Bowling Green.

In any event, in 1818 George Moore built himself a house at the then substantial cost of $4,000 and, with the essential help of his wife, Elizabeth, produced five children, all of whom moved away in the fullness of time except his daughter Mariah. Mariah never married and lived in the house that George built until her death in 1888. By that time, of course, the house was called Mariah Moore's house. In these less formal times it is called "Mariah's 1818."

The present proprietors, Rick Kelly and David Sears, converted it into a restaurant in 1979, opening up the space a bit but retaining as much as possible the original character of the house by preserving the original floor boards, restoring fireplace mantels and such. The menu is eclectic rather than traditional, with echoes of Italian and California cuisine. The owners have kindly permitted me to publish their recipes for Applesauce Muffins and Mariah's 1818 Cheesecake.

APPLESAUCE MUFFINS

1 cup (2 sticks) butter, at room temperature
2 cups sugar
2 eggs
3 teaspoons vanilla extract
4 cups all-purpose flour
2 teaspoons baking soda
1 tablespoon ground cinnamon
2 teaspoons ground allspice
1 teaspoon ground cloves
2 cups applesauce

Preheat the oven to 350°. Butter a 12-cup muffin tin, or use paper liners. In a large bowl, combine the butter, sugar, eggs and vanilla. Mix well. In another bowl, combine the flour, baking soda and spices. Add to the butter mixture and stir. Add the applesauce and mix very well.

Spoon the batter into the muffin tin. Bake for 20 to 25 minutes, until a cake tester inserted in the center of a muffin comes out dry and the muffins are lightly browned. Cool on a rack and remove the muffins from the pan. Repeat the process with the remaining batter.

Makes 2 dozen

MARIAH'S 1818 CHEESECAKE

CRUST:

2 cups graham cracker crumbs
¼ cup sugar
¼ cup melted butter

FILLING:

3 large packages (8 ounces each) cream cheese, at room temperature
1½ cups sugar
4 eggs
2 teaspoons vanilla extract
1 tablespoon fresh lemon juice

Grease an 8-inch springform pan. Mix together the crumbs, sugar and butter and press into the bottom of the pan.

Preheat the oven to 350°. Cream the cream cheese and sugar at high speed with an electric mixer. Reduce the speed to low and add the eggs one at a time. When all the eggs are beaten in, add the vanilla and lemon juice and mix thoroughly.

Pour into the crust and bake for 1 hour, until golden brown around the edges (the center may still be a bit loose). Cool on a rack for 3 to 4 hours. Run a knife around the edge of the pan and release the sides of the pan. Chill in the refrigerator until ready to serve.

Serves 12

Shaker Village, Pleasant Hill

The Shaker Village at Pleasant Hill, outside of Harrodsburg, is a remarkable place well worth a visit. The Shakers, so called because of the vigorous dances that were part of their religious practice, came with their founder, Mother Ann Lee, to the New World a few years before the American Revolution. They were a very distinctive people, gentle, ingenious and industrious, some of whose doctrines were decidedly eccentric. They spoke in tongues and required celibacy in their members; their buildings included separate entrances for men and women. Because there were no children born in the Shaker communities they raised orphans, allowing them to decide for themselves whether or not to become members of the community.

The Shakers prospered in America, living simply and frugally in accordance with their motto, "Hands to Work and Hearts to God." They established communities throughout New England and New York and eventually as far west as Kentucky, where they built the community in Pleasant Hill long known as Shakertown. They had a kind of genius in attending to the most ordinary everyday requirements, inventing such necessary and useful items as the wooden clothespin, the circular saw and the flat broom. Nested wooden boxes, dried herbs, garden seeds and household implements sold by the Shakers were the best available.

The Shakers had a remarkable design sense, achieving a kind of simple elegance in the creation of everyday objects that is unsurpassed. A Shaker tool or piece of furniture will at first seem utterly plain and utilitarian, until its grace and such a simple additional touch as the use of two differently grained woods or the introduction of a subtle curve or copper rivet reveals the Shaker craftsman's love for his work.

The same spirit informs the architecture of the Shakers, of which the buildings at Pleasant Hill are superb examples. There are today 27 restored buildings furnished throughout with authentic Shaker furniture, situated on 2,200 serenely beautiful acres at Pleasant Hill. The former communal houses provide lodging for visitors, while delicious food prepared in the Shaker tradition is served in the Pleasant Hill Dining Room in the restored Trustees' House, notable for its breathtaking twin circular staircases. The Shakers demonstrated a concern for nutrition far in advance of the general thinking of their day, emphasizing in particular the importance of fresh vegetables in the diet. They were also instrumental in promoting the use of herbs in American cooking.

These recipes are from two delightful books, *We Make You Kindly Welcome* and *Welcome Back to Pleasant Hill,* written by Elizabeth Kremer and published by Pleasant Hill, which kindly gave me permission to use them. These dishes are served in season at the Trustees' House, now the Pleasant Hill Dining Room.

TOMATO OKRA CASSEROLE

6 tablespoons chopped onions
2 tablespoons bacon fat
1 pound okra, trimmed and sliced into rounds
1 pound tomatoes, peeled and cooked or 1 quart canned
    tomatoes
1 tablespoon sugar
1½ teaspoons salt
½ teaspoon paprika
¼ teaspoon curry powder
¼ teaspoon cayenne pepper
2½ tablespoons grated Parmesan cheese
8 butter crackers (not saltines), crumbled

Preheat the oven to 350°. Butter a 9-inch glass or enameled baking dish. In a nonreactive skillet, sauté the onions in the hot bacon fat. Add the okra and cook until tender. Add the tomatoes, sugar and seasonings. Pour into the prepared baking dish. Top with the cheese and sprinkle with the cracker crumbs. Bake for 35 minutes, until bubbly.

Serves 12

BISQUE OF GARDEN PEAS

3 cups fresh peas (you may use frozen)
Pinch of salt
¼ cup chopped onions
3 tablespoons butter
3 tablespoons all-purpose flour
3 cups milk or half-and-half
Salt and cayenne pepper
Chopped mint leaves, for garnish

Cook the fresh peas in 2 cups of water with a pinch of salt until tender, or follow the package directions for frozen peas. Allow to cool slightly.

Combine the peas, their cooking liquid and the onions in a blender or food processor and blend until smooth.

In a large saucepan, melt the butter and stir in the flour until smooth and bubbly. Remove from the heat and slowly stir in the milk. Return to low heat, stirring constantly and cook until the sauce thickens. Add the puréed pea mixture and stir until blended. Season to taste with cayenne and salt. Chill until ready to serve. Garnish with chopped mint leaves.

Serves 6

STACK PIES

This is an extremely rich, early Kentucky recipe which evolved because cooks did not want to carry individual pies to reunions or camp meetings.

10 egg yolks
3 cups sugar
1 cup heavy cream
1½ cups melted butter
4 or 5 9-inch pie shells (page 60, double or triple the recipe)

Preheat the oven to 350°. Beat the egg yolks until light. Cream in the sugar. Add the cream and beat in the melted butter.

Leaving the pie shells in the pie pans, trim the crusts of all except the bottom crust just to the rim of the pie pan, making flat disks of dough. Leave the bottom pie crust intact. Pour the mixture into the shells, distributing evenly among the crusts. Bake until set, about 10 to 12 minutes. Cool the pies on a rack.

Remove all but the bottom pie from the pans and stack one on top of another. Cover with the caramel icing.

CARAMEL ICING:

½ cup (1 stick) butter
1 cup packed brown sugar
¼ cup milk or evaporated milk
2 cups confectioners' sugar

Melt the butter in a saucepan. Add the sugar and cook for 5 minutes, stirring constantly. Allow to cool slightly. Add the milk and beat until smooth. Stir in the confectioners' sugar.

Coat the top and sides of the stacked pie.

Serves about 24

Boone Tavern, Berea

Berea is located south of Lexington in the foothills of the Appalachian range. It is the home of Berea College, which owns and operates Boone Tavern as the college guest house. Berea is a very special college, privately endowed and devoted to providing higher education to the children of Appalachia, one of the most beautiful but poorest sections of the United States. Eighty percent of the student body is drawn from the mountains. Their tuition is defrayed in part by the school's endowment and gifts from admirers of this splendid institution. In addition, the students help pay the cost of their room and board through the school's unusual work/study program under which each student is required to work at least 10 hours each week in addition to carrying a full class load. One of the curriculum majors is hotel management, and almost all of the employees at Boone Tavern Hotel are Berea students. The friendliness, skill and youthful zeal of the staff makes staying or dining at Boone Tavern a very different experience from a visit to more impersonal hostelries.

The hotel began as a tin-roofed, 25-room facility 80 years ago, after Berea's president got tired of putting up visitors to the college in his own home. Since then it has been rather randomly added to and improved over the years. Today it houses 57 and includes a dining room that seats 200 in what has become a surprisingly graceful building set in the beautiful Berea campus.

Richard Hougen, who served as manager for 30 years, was an enthusiast for Southern cooking and an imaginative cook himself. His stewardship of the hotel brought the restaurant a national reputation, and his high standards for cooking and service continue to be maintained. The cookbooks he wrote are still available for sale at Boone Tavern, as are the restaurant's spoon bread mix and handmade products of Berea's Student Craft Industries, including wonderful textiles and ironwork. In fact, Berea is a great place to start collecting the lovely traditional handicrafts of the Appalachian mountaineers, since many craftspeople in pottery, quilting, weaving and woodworking, who employ techniques now almost vanished, market their products in this vicinity. Berea is also a good starting point for drives into the breathtakingly scenic Appalachian Mountains of eastern Kentucky.

Here are two recipes from the Boone Tavern Dining Room, one a rich creamed chicken served in a crisp potato basket, the other a beloved old chess pie named in honor of the Confederacy's president.

CHICKEN FLAKES IN A BIRD'S NEST

BIRDS' NESTS:

4 medium-sized potatoes
Vegetable oil for deep-frying

Heat the oil in a deep fryer to 350°. Peel and grate or shred the potatoes on a vegetable shredder with ⅜-inch round holes. Line a 4-inch in diameter strainer with the shredded potatoes, using only enough to thinly cover the inside of the strainer. Place a smaller, 2-inch in diameter strainer inside the first to hold the shredded potatoes in place.

Lower the nest into the hot, deep fat and fry until golden brown. Remove and tap or help the nest out of the bottom strainer by urging with the blade of a knife. Allow to cool. If made in advance, the nests can be reheated in the oven at 325° before filling with chicken flakes and sauce.

Makes 8

CHICKEN FLAKES IN CREAM SAUCE:

½ cup lard or a mixture of lard and butter
1 cup all-purpose flour
6 cups chicken stock
Salt and freshly ground pepper
4 cups cooked chicken, cut in ½-inch cubes or chunks

Melt the lard in the top of a double boiler over simmering water. Stir in the flour. Cook for 5 minutes, stirring constantly, to prevent sticking, until thickened. Meanwhile, heat the chicken stock. Add to the fat and flour and cook, stirring constantly, for 10 minutes, until thickened. Season to taste with salt and pepper. Stir the cubed chicken into the chicken cream sauce and heat through.

Add additional seasonings, if desired, and serve in the potato birds' nests.

Serves 8

JEFFERSON DAVIS PIE

2 cups packed brown sugar
1 tablespoon sifted all-purpose flour
½ teaspoon freshly grated nutmeg
1 cup heavy cream
4 eggs, lightly beaten
1 teaspoon fresh lemon juice
½ teaspoon grated lemon zest
½ cup (1 stick) melted butter
1 unbaked 9-inch pie shell (page 60)

Preheat the oven to 375°. In a bowl, sift together the sugar, flour and nutmeg. Add the cream and mix well. Add the eggs and mix well. Add the lemon juice, zest and melted butter. Beat well. Pour into the pie shell. Bake for 45 minutes, until a knife inserted into the pie comes out clean. Cool on a rack. Serve with whipped cream.

Serves 8

The Executive Mansion, Frankfort

Well, now, I recognize that the Governor's Mansion is far from being a public inn or restaurant, as you could probably prove for yourself by plopping down in the Governor's dining room and ordering a ham on rye. Nevertheless, it is a place of frequent entertaining, the tradition of hospitality in Kentucky being what it is. Governor Martha Layne Collins, Kentucky's first woman governor, has during her tenure constantly hosted formal and informal dinner parties, luncheons and even breakfasts, and, in addition, the enormous semi-public festivities connected with major celebrations like Derby Day.

Because Governor Collins has been kind enough to provide some of her recipes for this book, you will now be able to serve some of the same dishes offered the governor's guests.

BROWNIES

This recipe belongs to Governor Collins' mother-in-law, Mrs. Margaret Baker Collins of Versailles, formerly of Hazard, Kentucky. It has been in the Collins family for many years and has long been a favorite.

3 squares unsweetened chocolate
1 cup (2 sticks) butter
2 cups sugar
4 eggs, well beaten
1⅓ cups all-purpose flour
1 cup chopped pecans
Confectioners' sugar

Preheat the oven to 400°. Butter two 8-inch square baking pans. Melt the chocolate and butter in the top of a double boiler over simmering water. Remove from the heat and stir in the sugar. Allow to cool. Add the eggs, flour and pecans; stir well. Divide the batter between the prepared pans. Bake for about 18 minutes, until a tester comes out clean. Remove from the oven. Let cool for 10 minutes. Cut the contents of each pan into 36 brownies; immediately roll in confectioners' sugar. Let cool completely and store in a cake tin.

Makes 6 dozen

PEGASUS PIE

½ cup (1 stick) butter, cut into ½-inch cubes
1 cup sugar
1 cup light corn syrup
4 eggs
1 tablespoon bourbon whiskey
½ cup semisweet chocolate bits
1 cup chopped pecans
1 unbaked 9-inch pie shell (page 60)

Preheat the oven to 350°. In a bowl, combine all of the ingredients. Pour into the unbaked pie shell. Bake for 45 minutes, until a knife inserted into the pie comes out clean. Cool on a rack.

Serves 8

The Holidays

*T*he holidays in this section have little in common beyond the impatience with which I awaited them as a child and the heightened air of celebration they occasioned. I can recall a time when the intervals separating them seemed interminable, when Christmas seemed as remote to me on the Fourth of July as the Tudor era seems to me now. But this book is about remembering Kentucky and the wonderful foods we ate, each in its season, and nothing brings them more immediately to mind than imagining myself again on the way to church on Christmas Eve or walking down a sidewalk on a morning in early summer just before the grand occasion of the Fourth of July.

There are fence rows of honeysuckle scattered everywhere in the small towns of Kentucky and their perfume fills the July air. We used to pluck the blossoms, nip off the pointed tips with our teeth and suck out the piercingly sweet nectar that lodges in the very ends of the blossom bells—sometimes it has the flavor of strawberries, sometimes the flavor of melon. I've met people in the East with honeysuckle vines growing on their fences who never knew about sucking out the honey-like nectar. I don't know where they thought the name of the flower came from. It is so beloved back home that there is even a Honeysuckle Cotillion held every year at about prom time.

I remember early summer evenings in Kentucky when the sun set very late and dusk seemed to linger on and on, fading imperceptibly toward dark. Suddenly a single firefly would flicker into blinking glow, then another, and soon everywhere you looked there were magical flashes of soft greenish light. We kids would abandon our game of hide-and-seek, grab Mason jars and gallop across the lawns trying to capture the fireflies. It took speed, skill and luck since the light on the target always went out just before you got to it, and the insect always veered off in a new direction after switching off. You had to capture them in a loose fist and then thrust your hand into the jar to release the firefly without letting the earlier captives escape. We punched holes in the jar lids for ventilation, and I used to fall asleep gazing at the syncopated glow from the jar of fireflies on my bureau. The next day it was considered only sporting to release the survivors and go haring after a new set in the evening.

Each year as the Fourth of July approached, another sign of the season appeared at about the time the fireflies turned on. Sporadic machine-gun bursts from woven strings of firecrackers heralded the coming event, starting about a week in advance and increasing in frequency as the great day grew nearer. They were packaged in wondrous paper wrappings with an odd feel and texture, adorned with Chinese characters, dragons and distorted-looking American flags. When I got old enough to gain possession of firecrackers myself, I too was out at first darkness, a smoking punk in my hand, lighting long strings of tiny firecrackers or planting big individual ones under tin cans for the thrill of the deafening roar and the flight of the can up into the elm tree branches. Like the fireflies, I feel lucky now to have survived the experience.

The Fourth of July in Kentucky somehow has the feel of an earlier America, with bunting and parades and speeches, and children lining the streets waving miniature American flags. There are brass bands and raffles and contests of all kinds, and enough fire-crackers by day and fireworks displays by night to more than fulfill the Biblical injunction to make a joyful noise.

Independence Day is also celebrated by cooking and eating. Kentuckians turn out in great numbers to picnic in the country in such favorite spots as the banks of a lake or river, or they stay home and lay out a picnic spread on the screened-in porch. What-ever their surroundings, they are likely to serve some of the recipes in this chapter, making good use of the produce that is summer's bounty. They may also have hamburgers and hot dogs on the grill, but you already know how to cook them. Here are some other dishes with which to celebrate American Independence.

TEA PUNCH

Abraham Lincoln once took a taste from the cup handed him and said politely, "If this is coffee, please bring me some tea; if this is tea, please bring me some coffee." This has nothing to do with this refreshing, non-alcoholic punch, but I thought you might like to hear it since he was Kentucky's only native-born president.

¼ cup sugar
Zest and juice of 2 lemons
Zest and juice of 2 oranges
1 teaspoon whole cloves
1 cinnamon stick
2 tablespoons orange pekoe tea

In a saucepan, combine 4 cups water with the sugar, lemon and orange zests, cloves and cinnamon. Bring to a boil and boil for 10 minutes. Remove from the heat. Add the tea and let steep for 3 minutes. Strain and dilute with 2 cups water. Add the lemon and orange juices just before serving either hot or cold.

Serves 6

HAM MOUSSE

This dish is as elegant as any cold dish I know of but it can be made from the leftover scraps of a country ham, which are far too good to be thrown away. By making a mousse you don't have to try to make little bits of ham look nice on a platter. And the mousse is good enough to justify using a new ham if you don't have leftovers.

2 envelopes unflavored gelatin
1⅓ cups chicken broth
2 eggs, separated
3½ cups ground or minced cooked ham (preferably country ham)
1 cup heavy cream

Sprinkle the gelatin over ¼ cup water to soften it. Heat the chicken broth until almost boiling. Lightly beat the egg yolks. Stir in a little of the heated broth to warm them. Pour the egg yolks into the broth and cook over low heat for a few minutes, until thickened. Add the gelatin and cook, stirring, until dissolved. Add the ham.

Beat the egg whites until stiff. Whip the heavy cream. Fold the egg whites and cream into the mousse and blend well. Mold and refrigerate until firm.

Serves 6 to 8

CRAB SALAD

This crab salad is made with a green herb mayonnaise that adds color and flavor, without overwhelming the delicate flavor of the crab. Make this salad just before you plan to serve it.

10 parsley sprigs
4 tarragon sprigs
½ cup chopped spinach
1¼ cups mayonnaise
3 tablespoons heavy cream
2 teaspoons fresh lemon juice
Salt and freshly ground pepper
6 ounces cooked crabmeat, picked over and flaked
2 large ripe avocados, or 4 large lettuce leaves

Cook the parsley, tarragon and spinach in a small quantity of boiling, salted water until just tender, 5 to 8 minutes. Drain well and squeeze dry. Purée through a sieve or in an electric blender. Gently fold the purée into the mayonnaise. Add the cream and lemon juice; season with salt and pepper to taste. Fold in the crabmeat.

Serve in halved avocados or on lettuce leaves.

Serves 4

CUCUMBER ASPIC

This recipe, like the tomato-flavored Vegetable Aspic in the Traditional Specialties chapter (page 48) is a cooling, shimmery, welcome way to enjoy your vegetables during hot spells. Either one, red or green, supplies a nice note of color on the table, and a cucumber aspic is even cooler than a cucumber which, as you know, is notoriously cool.

1 cup coarsely chopped, peeled and seedless cucumber
½ cup chopped green bell pepper
2 medium onions, chopped
2 tablespoons minced fresh dill
3 tablespoons tarragon vinegar
2 envelopes unflavored gelatin
1 cup boiling water
Salt and freshly ground pepper
Dill sprigs, for garnish

Combine the cucumber, bell pepper, onions and dill in a food processor and purée. Stir in the vinegar.

In a metal measuring cup, stir the gelatin into ¼ cup of water. Heat in a pan of simmering water until the gelatin softens. Add the boiling water and stir until the gelatin dissolves.

Stir the gelatin mixture into the cucumber purée. Season with salt and pepper to taste. Transfer to a 2-cup mold or bowl or to individual ½-cup molds. Refrigerate and chill until set. Garnish with dill sprigs.

Serves 4

FANNIE BELL'S FRIED CHICKEN

Fannie Bell Weaver was a famous Louisville cook known for her party catering. One of her ancestors, a slave in Bardstown, served Louis Philippe when he was in exile there. I can't say whether Louis Philippe enjoyed this fried chicken recipe, but everyone I've ever served it to has. Serve hot or cold.

2-pound fryer chicken, cut up
½ cup all-purpose flour
1 teaspoon paprika
1 teaspoon salt
2 teaspoons freshly ground black pepper
1 pound lard or 1½ inches vegetable oil
½ cup (1 stick) butter

Wash the chicken and pat dry. Combine the flour, paprika, salt and pepper in a shallow dish. Thoroughly coat each piece of chicken with the mixture. Heat the lard and butter in a heavy cast-iron skillet over high heat until smoking hot.

Place the chicken in the hot fat and cook for 5 minutes on each side. Reduce the heat to moderately low, cover and cook slowly, turning frequently, until the chicken is golden brown and tender, about 15 minutes on each side. As each piece is done, place it on a brown paper bag on a baking sheet in a warm oven to keep chicken hot and to drain off excess cooking oil. When all of the chicken is cooked, remove to a hot platter and serve.

Serves 4 to 6

STRAWBERRY SHORTCAKE

I've enjoyed many kinds of shortcake. The fruit used can be sweet berries or peaches, ripe plums or cherries. And the "cake" can be a pound cake, a sponge cake or a biscuit (try the Cream of Tartar Biscuit recipe on page 57).

My favorite shortcake recipe, however, is this easy, wonderfully rich Austrian pastry shortened with butter and cream cheese and buried in an abundance of juicy red strawberries and whipped cream.

½ cup (1 stick) butter, at room temperature
1 small package (3 ounces) cream cheese, at room temperature
1 cup sifted all-purpose flour
2 pints strawberries, 6 whole berries reserved for garnish, the remainder hulled and sliced
5 tablespoons sugar
1 teaspoon vanilla extract
1 cup heavy cream

Preheat the oven to 325°. Cream together the butter and cream cheese. Mix in the flour. Place the dough on a floured board and pat into a ½-inch-thick disk. With a floured rolling pin, roll out ¼ inch thick. Cut into desired shapes: these 3-inch rounds are ideal for individual servings, or use two 4-inch layers per person. If the dough is too soft, refrigerate it for 10 to 15 minutes. It should roll out beautifully. Place the rounds on a baking sheet. Bake for 20 to 25 minutes, until lightly browned. Cool on a rack.

Gently toss 4 tablespoons of the sugar with the sliced berries. Cover and set aside to become juicy. Stir the remaining 1 tablespoon sugar and the vanilla into the heavy cream. Whip until the cream forms soft mounds.

When the pastry has cooled, heap a layer of berries on a pastry round, top with a second round and heap more berries on it. Top with a third round and mound that with berries. Top the berries with the whipped cream. Add a single, perfect whole berry in the center.

Serves 6

SUMMER PUDDING LAFAYETTE

This pudding is forever engraved in my memory as one of the delights of summer. It is simplicity itself to cook, but it takes a jigsaw puzzler's skills to assemble it. (Jigsaw puzzles are one of the delights of winter.) Use a good, firm bread; all-American commercial sponge-and-air bread won't do. A good French bread has the body necessary to hold together. Perhaps that is why the name of Lafayette is attached to this luscious dessert.

**3 pounds mixed berries (any combination of raspberries, black-
    berries, strawberries, blueberries or red currants)**
**1 cup sugar, depending on the sweetness of the berries (2 cups if
    a heavy portion of cranberries or red currants is used)**
10 slices firm, fresh white bread

Clean and wash the fruit thoroughly. Place in a nonreactive saucepan over a low heat. Add sugar gradually, stirring until dissolved.

Butter a 1-quart pudding bowl. Line the bottom and sides with 7 slices of bread, trimming to fit together with no gaps between the seams. Pour the fruit mixture over the bread. Cover the top with the 3 remaining slices of bread fitting close together as before. Cover the bowl with a flat plate that fits neatly inside the rim and put a heavy weight on top of the plate. Refrigerate overnight.

Before serving, remove the plate and run a knife around the inside of the bowl. Invert the pudding onto a large serving dish.

Serves 6

HOMEMADE VANILLA ICE CREAM

Making your own ice cream is not an economical measure. You can buy ice cream cheaper than you can make it, and making ice cream can be a lot of trouble. Nevertheless, I and lots of other people continue to make ice cream whenever the chance presents itself simply because it is infinitely better than the best ice cream you can buy. Besides, I still get a nostalgic thrill remembering those blue, green and gold afternoons under the old trees when my aunts would mix up the custard and fill the galvanized quart-size container, attach the dasher, place it in the wooden outer bucket and pack in cracked ice and rock salt. Then James Miller Williams and I would take turns revolving the crank to churn air into the freezing mixture and keep it from turning into a block of ice. The crank would get harder and harder to turn, and the anticipation would get harder and harder to bear as the ice cream froze. At last James and my aunts would give the crank handle a final turn or two, confer briefly and pronounce the ice cream ready. James and I would disassemble the mechanism and I always was given the dasher to lick as assistant crank-turner's prerogative. Today all of this can be done very simply with the new ice cream freezers available. The process is less memorable but the product is just as good.

"Plain vanilla ice cream" is an expression these days for an oversweet boring blandness, but real homemade vanilla is the finest ice cream ever made. It almost assaults the tongue with a delirious combination of sweet, crisp coldness, the exotic perfume from the vanilla bean and the lusciousness of sweet cream.

6 egg yolks
2 cups milk
1 cup sugar
1 teaspoon salt
**1 vanilla bean, split lengthwise, or 2 tablespoons pure vanilla
      extract**
2 cups heavy cream

In the top of a double boiler, off the heat, whisk the egg yolks and milk until well blended. Stir in the sugar, salt and vanilla bean (if you are using it). Cook, stirring constantly, over hot but not boiling water, until thick and creamy. Remove from the heat and allow to cool. Cover and refrigerate until chilled.

Remove the vanilla bean and scrape the brown flecks into the chilled custard mixture, or stick in the vanilla extract. Pour the mixture into the container of an ice cream maker and freeze until partially frozen and mushy. Whip the heavy cream until soft peaks form. At this point, if your freezer container is not large enough to incorporate the whipped cream, pour the custard mixture into a chilled bowl. Beat the mixture until smooth and creamy, and then fold in the whipped cream. Blend well. Pour the mixture back into the freezer container. Cover and freeze until firm.

Serve with a favorite topping.

Makes 1 quart

PEPPERMINT ICE CREAM:

Vanilla ice cream (page 181), partially frozen
1 cup finely chopped peppermint stick candy

About 5 minutes before you expect the vanilla ice cream to be finished, add the chopped peppermint stick candy to the container and continue to crank till frozen.

PEACH ICE CREAM:

2 cups coarsely chopped, peeled and stoned ripe peaches
¼ cup superfine sugar
2 tablespoons fresh lemon juice
Vanilla ice cream (page 181), partially frozen

Combine the peaches and their juice with the sugar and lemon juice. Cover and let stand for at least 10 minutes. Add to the partially frozen vanilla ice cream for the last 5 minutes or so of cranking.

Makes 1 quart

Some Simple Sundae Sauces

Here are five toppings for ice cream. They are quickly and easily made and are better than store-bought, particularly the berry sauce, which contains both cooked and uncooked fruit, and the pecan sauce, which is crowded with freshly butter-toasted pecans. These richly flavored toppings are best used on plain vanilla ice cream.

PECAN SAUCE

4 tablespoons butter
1 cup pecans
¾ cup brown or white sugar
½ cup light corn syrup
½ teaspoon salt

Preheat the oven to 350°. In a cake pan, combine 3 tablespoons of the butter and the pecans. Place in the hot oven and toast, stirring frequently, until the pecans are heated through and well coated, 15 to 20 minutes. Remove and let cool.

In a saucepan, combine the sugar, corn syrup and salt. Bring to a boil and boil for about 5 minutes. Chop the pecans and stir into the syrup along with the remaining 1 tablespoon butter and the vanilla. Serve hot or cold.

Makes about 2 cups

BERRY SAUCE

1½ cups strawberries, cherries, blackberries or a combination
½ cup superfine sugar
½ teaspoon salt
1 cup boiling water
2 tablespoons fresh lemon juice

In a saucepan, combine 1 cup of the berries, the sugar, salt and boiling water. Boil for 2 to 3 minutes. Turn off the heat and stir in the lemon juice and remaining ½ cup berries.

Makes 1½ cups

RUM SAUCE

¾ cup sugar
½ cup light corn syrup
½ teaspoon salt
3 tablespoons butter
¼ cup dark rum

In a saucepan, boil the sugar, corn syrup and salt for about 5 minutes. Stir in the butter and rum. Serve hot or cold.

Makes about 1 cup

CHOCOLATE SAUCE

2 squares unsweetened chocolate
1 cup sugar
2 tablespoons dark corn syrup
2 tablespoons butter

In a saucepan, melt the chocolate over low heat. Add the sugar, corn syrup, butter and ⅓ cup water. Cook for 5 minutes over moderate heat, stirring occasionally.

Makes about 1 cup

KENTUCKY SAUCE

This is a multipurpose dessert sauce for grown-ups. It is a perfect topping for homemade vanilla ice cream, is grand on pound cake and can even be used to enhance fresh strawberries. It keeps well and, put up in glass jars, makes a nice stocking stuffer at Christmastime.

½ cup packed brown sugar
½ cup granulated sugar
1 cup strawberry preserves
Juice and grated zest of 1 orange
Juice and grated zest of 1 lemon
1 cup bourbon whiskey
1 cup chopped pecans

Combine the brown and white sugars with 1 cup water and the preserves in a saucepan. Bring to a boil and cook until the mixture spins a thread, or until a little of the mixture forms a heavy thread a couple of inches long when poured from a spoon. Remove from the heat and add the orange and lemon juice. Add 1 teaspoon each of the grated lemon and orange zests along with the bourbon and chopped pecans. Refrigerate until chilled.

Makes 4 cups

PEACH COBBLER

The sensuous appeal of fully ripe peaches makes them an irresistible part of end-of-summer dining. I considered putting in a recipe
for peach pie here, but the technique is similar to apple pie, which
is included elsewhere. Instead, here is a peach cobbler that is easier
to make than pie, has the same union of fruit and pastry crust and
is a taste of heaven on earth when served warm with thick cream.

⅔ **cup sugar**
1½ cups plus 1 tablespoon all-purpose flour
4 cups fresh peach slices
6 tablespoons (¾ stick) butter, cut into bits
¾ teaspoon ground cinnamon
1 tablespoon baking powder
¼ teaspoon salt
3 tablespoons lard
About ½ cup milk

Combine the sugar and the 1 tablespoon flour in a saucepan.
Add the peaches and cook over low heat, stirring constantly, until
the fruit is tender, about 5 minutes. Pour into an 8-inch square
pan. Dot with the butter and sprinkle with the cinnamon.

Preheat the oven to 425°. Sift together the remaining 1½ cups
flour, the baking powder and salt. Add the lard and mix in with a
pastry blender. With a fork, stir in milk, using only enough to
soften the dough. Transfer to a lightly floured board and knead for
5 seconds. Roll into a 9-inch square about ½ inch thick. Place on
top of the peaches, pinching the dough to the rim of the pan. Bake
for 25 to 30 minutes, or until browned. Serve warm with or without
cream.

Serves 6

Christmas

In most households in Kentucky—as in homes everywhere—
Christmas Eve is a busy time. Some families decorate the tree on
Christmas Eve; others exchange presents then. In households with
little children, it is necessary to get some food into the overexcited

next generation, keep it reasonably civil and pack it off to bed. (It is not considered good form to serve gin-and-laudanum nightcaps to toddlers; you must quiet them some other way.) Then there are all those preparations for the next morning to be got into place as if by magic. Maybe you're good at magic. If not, you'll just have to get by on sheer nervous energy. There are the presents that still need to be wrapped and, in my family, Christmas Eve services at church. We used to stick the last bit of tape on the last present, slick down our hair, pull on coats and scarves, and hurry out through the chilly night air and down the street to the First Presbyterian Church. (I always felt a little like a traitor to my Baptist grandmother, who was not only a pillar of the church and the Sunday school superintendent but oversaw the Christmas decorations for her church.) Nevertheless, it was off to services with the Presbyterian Pattesons.

The church was always filled with banks of poinsettias and evergreen boughs and the scent of pine mingled with incense and the women's perfume. It was amazing how many familiar faces were there, some of whom one hadn't seen since last Easter. After services the family and sometimes friends who had no one with whom to share the holidays would all go back to our house for a midnight supper.

For an occasion like this, your menu should consist of foods that can be heated and served in short order. The guests should have time to share a drink or two and a little conversation, and then supper should be on the table without reducing the host or hostess to jelly. The holidays are sufficiently complicated without making the preparation of food at the beginning of the season a daunting prospect. So here are some dishes that are warming, satisfying, festive, cheerful and easy to prepare in advance or toss together at the last minute.

Christmas Eve Midnight Supper

LENTIL SOUP

Hearty and nourishing, lentil soup is beloved by practically everyone. It's a good dish for Christmas Eve supper because it can be made well in advance and reheated after you get home from services. You might also consider serving it on New Year's Eve—for luck. If, as I am told, a Jewish tradition holds that each lentil you eat at New Year's will produce a gold coin in the coming year, you can very easily double this recipe. *Mazel tov!*

2 cups dried lentils, picked over
10 cups boiling water
1 large onion, pierced with 2 or 3 cloves
¼ pound salt pork, a piece of ham or a ham bone
3 tablespoons butter
1 medium onion, minced
¼ teaspoon dried thyme
1 bay leaf
Freshly ground pepper

Wash the lentils and drain. Place in a large saucepan and add the boiling water, the whole onion and salt pork. Simmer for about 4 hours. Remove the whole onion and discard it. Melt the butter in a small skillet. Add the minced onion and sauté for a few minutes until translucent. Add the onion, thyme and bay leaf to the soup. Cook for 1 hour. Season with pepper before serving.

Serves 8

SCALLOPED OYSTERS

I'm very fond of scalloped oysters, and not alone in this enthusiasm. In winter there is nothing more warming and comforting than a bubbly, creamy dish of oysters covered with a golden brown crust of crumbs. This dish is quick and easy to prepare and very versatile, serving equally well as a side dish at dinner or as the main course for a luncheon.

1 pint shucked oysters with their liquor
½ cup light cream
½ cup day-old bread crumbs

1 cup cracker crumbs
½ cup (1 stick) butter, melted
Salt and freshly ground pepper
½ teaspoon ground mace
Paprika

Preheat the oven to 425°. Butter a 1-quart casserole or baking dish. Drain the oysters, reserving ¼ cup of the liquor. Combine the oyster liquor with the cream in a bowl and set aside. Mix both kinds of crumbs together with the melted butter and sprinkle a thin layer on the bottom of the casserole. Cover with half of the oysters, half of the liquor and cream mixture and a light sprinkling of salt and pepper. Cover with half of the remaining crumbs, the remaining oysters, the remaining liquor and cream and more salt and pepper. Finish off the dish with the last of the crumbs and sprinkle with the mace and paprika. (Keep the dish shallow as more than 2 layers of oysters will cause the middle layer to remain uncooked.) Bake for 30 minutes, until bubbly.

Serves 4

CRABMEAT THERMIDOR

This dish is named after lobster thermidor, which it somewhat resembles. That well-known lobster dish was named by Napoleon for the month in which it was first served to him. (The month of Thermidor, meaning gift of heat, started in late August and was so designated by the National Convention following the French Revolution. Like legislators everywhere, the participants of this new assembly were casting about for things to improve or at least change. Thus, they renamed and redated the months, apparently to inform people what the weather was likely to be.)

This recipe calls for crabmeat in a sherried cream sauce.

4 tablespoons (½ stick) butter
1 small onion, minced
2 tablespoons all-purpose flour
2 cups heavy cream
½ teaspoon salt
½ teaspoon freshly ground white pepper
1½ pounds cooked crabmeat or king crab legs, cut up
2 tablespoons amontillado sherry

Melt the butter in a heavy skillet. Add the onion and cook until translucent. Whisk in the flour and mix well. In a saucepan, bring the cream, salt and pepper just to a simmer. Add to the onion all at once, whisking vigorously until thickened. Stir in the crabmeat. Add the sherry just before serving.

Serve hot, over rice.

Serves 8

VEAL AND SWEETBREADS PIE

This pie is filled with very tender and delicately flavored meats, gently cooked and lightly spiced to avoid overwhelming the subtleties of the main ingredients. It is enjoyed for its luxurious richness.

½ pound veal sweetbreads
2 teaspoons vinegar or lemon juice
¾ pound veal tenderloin, cubed
¼ cup (½ stick) butter
1 cup boiling water
½ cup diced potato
¼ cup diced carrot
¼ cup diced celery
8 small white onions
1 bay leaf
1 teaspoon salt
2 tablespoons cornstarch
1 teaspoon ground mace
1 egg, separated
Dough for 2 lard pie crusts (page 60)

Soak the sweetbreads in cold water to cover for at least 1 hour. Drain and soak again. Drain well. Place the sweetbreads in a saucepan of cold water with the vinegar. Bring to a simmer and cook for 2 to 5 minutes. Drain, cover with cold water and drain again. Trim off any tubes, membranes and cartilage. All of this can be done well in advance.

Preheat the oven to 425°. In a heavy cast-iron skillet, sauté the veal cubes in the butter. Add the boiling water, potato, carrot, celery, onions, bay leaf and salt. Cook for 5 minutes. Remove the veal and vegetables. Stir the cornstarch into ¼ cup water. Thicken the gravy in the skillet with the cornstarch. Return the veal, sweetbreads, vegetables and mace to the skillet.

Line a 3-quart casserole or soufflé dish with the lard pie crust, saving enough for an overlapping top crust. Fill the casserole with the meat mixture. Top with the remaining dough and crimp the overlapping crusts together. Slash the top crust in several places to allow steam to escape and brush with the egg white. Bake for 30 minutes. Brush the crust with the beaten egg yolk and bake for 5 minutes more, until browned. The pie can be assembled in advance and put into the oven a half hour or so before serving.

Serves 6 to 8

BOILED CUSTARD

Only in Kentucky have I seen this very soft custard that is the consistency of cream. My cousin, Elizabeth Sanders, who is famous for her lavish Christmas entertaining, serves the custard in antique sterling punch cups. She passes a small cut-glass pitcher of fine bourbon to let guests add what they wish, although the custard is delicious without added spirits. It can also be made in the caramel variation that follows this recipe. She serves slices of Prune Cake (page 192) along with it.

4 egg yolks
½ cup sugar
2 cups milk, scalded
Pinch of salt
1 teaspoon vanilla extract

In the top of a double boiler, whisk the egg yolks until thick and lemon-colored. Whisk in the sugar, then slowly pour the hot milk over the mixture as you stir. Place over simmering water and stir constantly with a wooden spoon for 5 to 10 minutes, until the custard coats the spoon. Remove from the heat at once and add the salt and vanilla.

NOTE: If you have a candy thermometer, cook the custard to 165°.
   Variations: For Caramel Boiled Custard, substitute brown sugar for the white sugar in the basic recipe.
For Custard Sauce, follow the recipe for the regular or caramel versions but use 2 egg yolks instead of 4.

Serves 4

MILDRED EMERSON'S CHRISTMAS COOKIES

I remember my childhood job of going down to the cellar a week before Christmas with the important assignment of shelling a sack of hazelnuts by placing each on a brick and hitting it with a hammer. The object was to crack the shell but avoid pulverizing the nut. I became fairly skillful at it, although not without a fair number of misplaced blows. Still, it was well worth the price of a few painful misses to sample these delicate, crumbly little cookies that combine the warmth of butter and nuts with the delightful sensation of the thick layer of powdered sugar. Because hazelnuts have gotten scarcer than hen's teeth, this recipe calls for pecans, which are different but also wonderful. And, as Mildred Emerson said in a note to herself on her recipe card, "Very easy to make."

1 cup (2 sticks) butter, at room temperature
⅓ cup confectioners' sugar (plus more to coat the cookies)
1¾ cups sifted all-purpose flour
1 teaspoon vanilla extract
1½ cups chopped pecans or hazelnuts

In a bowl, cream the butter with the sugar. Add all of the remaining ingredients and mix well. Divide in half and form into two long rolls, each 1½ to 2 inches wide. Wrap individually in waxed paper and refrigerate overnight or until very firm.

Preheat the oven to 350°. Cut the cookie rolls into ¼-inch slices. Place on a baking sheet. Bake for 10 to 12 minutes, until lightly browned.

While still warm, sprinkle generously with additional confectioners' sugar.

Makes about 4 dozen

PRUNE CAKE

Despite the name, this cake doesn't taste much like prunes. It is a very moist, dense cake with the flavor of spices and an elusive aftertaste of chocolate. The fruit element is there but not easy to identify. Nevertheless, this cake, although mysterious, is delicious, particularly with Boiled Custard (page 191), whipped cream or Lemon Sauce (page 133).

2 cups cake flour
1 teaspoon baking soda
1 teaspoon salt
1 teaspoon ground allspice
1 teaspoon ground cloves
2 tablespoons unsweetened cocoa powder
1 cup granulated sugar
1 cup packed brown sugar
1 cup vegetable oil
3 eggs
1 cup buttermilk
1 cup chopped pecans
1 cup mashed cooked prunes

Preheat the oven to 350°. Butter a tube pan. Sift together the flour, soda, salt, spices and cocoa. In a bowl, combine the sugars and vegetable oil. Beat the eggs into the buttermilk.

Beat the dry ingredients into the sugar and oil mixture. Fold in the egg mixture. Fold in the nuts and prunes.

Pour into the prepared pan and bake for 1 hour and 15 minutes, until a toothpick inserted in the center comes out clean. Cool briefly in the pan before inverting on to a rack to cool completely.

Serve with a cup of Boiled Custard and/or sweetened whipped cream.

Serves 10 to 12

Christmas Dinner

It doesn't always snow back home at Christmas—we may have snow one year out of three—but everyone prays for a storybook Christmas out of Dickens. In fact, we probably have more white Christmases in Kentucky than Dickens ever saw. The English Christmas seems to run more to drizzle than drifts; I've seen roses in bloom in London during Christmas week.

Snow or no, however, the Christmas traditions are deeply rooted in Kentucky, and Christmas dinner is the centerpiece of holiday entertaining. The main course is always a roast—simply the best way to serve a large number of people. A large roast lends itself to the most impressive presentation, and it is also, *mirabile dictu*, the easiest entrée to prepare for a throng. There is the usual variety of opinion as to the right roast for Christmas. Both turkey and goose have large, enthusiastic followings, and this being Kentucky, ham is, of course, the choice of a sizable minority. There may also be those who prefer lamb or roast pork, but for me the obvious choice is roast beef. It is too soon after Thanksgiving to get excited over turkey, and goose is a lot of trouble. To me, nothing is as delicious as a perfectly cooked standing rib roast of beef, the focal point of the following traditional Christmas dinner menu.

STANDING RIB ROAST OF BEEF

Roasts are the easiest way to cook for a lot of people. They are also delicious and impressive and just about the most impressive of all is the standing rib roast of beef. When you serve a standing rib roast, you will be praised for doing a superb job of cooking, when, in fact, you have had to do little more than heat the oven, shove the roast in and close the oven door. It helps to make up for those times when you have cooked something intricate and wonderful and everyone takes it for granted. And difficult or not, a standing rib roast tastes magnificent.

There are many approaches to roasting beef. They include, for example, putting the roast in a very hot oven (over 500°) for a short time to sear the roast and then turning off the heat and letting the roast sit (*without opening the oven door*) for a few hours. I hesitate to recommend this technique (although it can work beautifully), because not every oven is insulated well enough to hold heat for the necessary amount of time. Other methods include searing the meat for a period, reducing the temperature to the internal temperature you want the meat to be when done (e.g., 125° for medium rare) and leaving it in the oven at that temperature for 24 hours. Or you can roast the beef at a continuous low temperature, e.g., 250° or 300° until done. This has the advantage of reducing shrinkage and produces a roast uniformly cooked throughout but at the cost of some flavor since the outside does not brown, crisp or caramelize and diners don't have a choice as to how well done they want their cut. This is the way I roast beef:

8-pound standing rib roast, chine removed
Light vegetable oil
Thyme, rosemary or garlic clove (optional)

Remove the roast from the refrigerator 2 hours before you plan to cook it. Rub a little vegetable oil on the meat. Rub with thyme, rosemary or a cut garlic clove if desired. Do not salt.

Preheat the oven to 500°. Place the roast, fat side up, in a large shallow roasting pan. No rack is necessary. Insert a meat thermometer (if you use the type that remains in the meat) into the center of the lean meat, making sure it does not touch fat or bone or rest on the edge of the roasting pan.

Put the roast in the oven for 25 minutes. Reduce the oven temperature to 350° and continue to roast until done, about 20 minutes per pound. Keep your eye on the thermometer and if you use the instant reading sort, start checking the temperature after the meat has cooked about 16 minutes per pound (about 2 hours for an 8-pound roast).

When the internal temperature reaches 125° (for medium rare), remove the roast from the oven and let it rest for 15 to 30 minutes. The temperature will continue to rise after the roast is out of the oven and this gives the juices a chance to settle before carving the roast.

Place on a serving platter and garnish with watercress or parsley and crabapples or cherry tomatoes. Carve at the table. If the center of the roast is medium rare, which most people seem to prefer, there will nevertheless be well-done and medium servings available at the outside of the roast.

Serves 10 to 12

HORSERADISH SAUCE OR MOLD

Horseradish lends just the right touch of piquancy to roast beef. It can be served in the form of a creamy sauce or firmed up into a mold. If you can get fresh horseradish by all means use it, grating it at the last minute into a little lemon juice and preparing the sauce just before you plan to serve it. Usually, you will have to use prepared horseradish, which is sold in bottles and kept refrigerated.

Serve this sprightly, highly flavored sauce in the molded form with roast beef, seafood or marinated vegetables. I sometimes serve it as a garnish, using small molds and unmolding each on a thick slice of avocado, topping the mold with chopped parsley or with crossed pimiento strips. It is excellent in the form of a sauce on cold vegetables and on cold roast beef.

1½ tablespoons prepared horseradish
1 teaspoon onion juice
2 teaspoons white wine vinegar
½ teaspoon dry mustard
1 teaspoon salt
1 cup sour cream
½ cup mayonnaise
1 envelope unflavored gelatin
½ cup cold water

In a bowl, blend together the horseradish, onion juice, vinegar, mustard and salt to form a smooth paste. Mix thoroughly with the sour cream and mayonnaise. This mixture, omitting the gelatin and water, is horseradish sauce.

To make the horseradish mold, soften the gelatin in the cold water. Dissolve over hot water and beat into the sauce. Pour into an oiled 2-cup mold and chill.

Makes 2 cups

CREAMED ONIONS

I love the flavor of creamed onions with roast beef. Cutting a small cross in the root of each onion will help keep it from separating during cooking.

24 small white onions, peeled and scored at the root end
2 tablespoons butter
2 tablespoons all-purpose flour
1 cup half-and-half
½ teaspoon salt
Pinch of ground cloves
¼ cup chopped fresh parsley

Cover the onions with cold salted water and bring to a boil in a small saucepan. Reduce the heat and simmer until the onions are fork-tender. Drain.

Melt the butter in a saucepan and gradually add the flour. Stir until smooth. Cook over low heat for several minutes. Stir in the half-and-half and cook, stirring constantly, until the sauce is smooth and bubbly.

Remove from the heat and stir in the salt, cloves and parsley. Stir the onions into the sauce and serve.

Serves 4 to 6

POPOVERS

A popover is a large bubble of warm air surrounded by a crispy, chewy shell of crust. A cream puff shell is much the same and, in fact, if you have any left over, these popovers can be filled like a cream puff with boiled custard to make an easy dessert.

I like to serve popovers instead of Yorkshire pudding with roast beef. Yorkshire pudding made with the beef drippings was developed to help make roast beef serve more people, and is a very tasty dish in its own right. However, if you have plenty of roast for your guests, popovers are easier to make, provide a similar crunchy bread and don't require as much last-minute attention.

1 cup sifted all-purpose flour
½ teaspoon salt
2 eggs
1 cup milk
3 tablespoons butter, melted

Preheat the oven to 425°. Grease muffin or popover pans and set in the oven to preheat.

Combine all of the ingredients in a bowl and beat until smooth. Fill the cups slightly less than half full. Bake for 35 minutes. Do not open the oven door during baking. Have faith. Serve immediately.

Serves 6

CRANBERRY MOLD (CHRISTMAS STAR)

In my family, we always called this cranberry salad "Christmas Star" because it was made in a star-shaped mold that had been in the pantry as long as anyone could remember. This sweet salad is, of course, a lovely, warming red color and, in my opinion, a real improvement over plain cranberry sauce, which often tends to be a little too tart. The nuts and celery give it crunch, and it serves as a good foil for any of the rich meats usually served during the holidays—turkey, goose, roast beef or suckling pig.

2 envelopes unflavored gelatin
1 cup fresh orange juice
2 cups cranberries
½ cup sugar
¼ teaspoon salt
⅔ cup diced celery
½ cup chopped nuts
1 cup drained canned crushed pineapple
2 tablespoons grated orange zest

Soften the gelatin in 3 tablespoons of water. In a nonreactive saucepan, bring the orange juice to a boil. Add the cranberries and cook until their skins pop. (You may use the cranberries strained or unstrained depending on the texture you prefer. If you wish to strain the berries, do so at this point.) Add the sugar and salt and cook for 5 minutes. Add the softened gelatin and stir to dissolve completely. Chill.

When the mixture is almost set, fold in the remaining ingredients. Rinse a 6-cup mold and while still wet, fill with the mixture. Chill until firm. Serve with a mayonnaise sauce.

Serves 6 to 8

MA KATE EBLEN'S CINNAMON ROLLS

This versatile recipe can be used to produce scrumptious cinnamon rolls or, without the cinnamon topping, a delicate, slightly sweet bread roll, shaped either as a cloverleaf or the familiar Parker House roll. (At home we referred to them as "pocketbook rolls.") Instructions for the variations follow the sweet roll recipe.

ROLLS:

1 cup milk
¼ cup lard
¼ cup sugar
1 teaspoon salt
1 egg
1 package (¼ ounce) active dry yeast
3⅔ cups cake flour

CINNAMON MIXTURE:

⅓ cup butter
1 cup packed light brown sugar
2 teaspoons ground cinnamon

Make the rolls: Scald the milk in a saucepan. Add the lard, sugar and salt and stir well. Allow to cool to lukewarm.

In a large bowl, beat the egg with the milk mixture. Add the yeast and beat until dissolved. Add 2 cups of the flour and beat until very smooth. Add ⅔ cup more flour and beat until very smooth. Stir in the remaining 1 cup flour by hand, until smooth. Cover the bowl with a towel and let the dough rise in a warm place until doubled in bulk.

Meanwhile, make the cinnamon mixture: melt the butter. Stir in the brown sugar and cinnamon. Set aside.

When the dough is risen, divide it in half. Roll out one portion of dough into a 12 x 8-inch rectangle. Spread with half of the cinnamon mixture. Starting at a long end, roll up like a jelly roll, pressing firmly as you roll. Slice into 12 pieces and place, sides touching, in a buttered 9-inch round cake pan. Roll out the second piece of dough and proceed as before. Let rise in a warm place until doubled in bulk.

Preheat the oven to 400°. Bake the rolls for about 12 minutes, until lightly browned. Serve warm. The rolls can be reheated.

For Pocketbook Rolls: After the dough has risen and doubled in bulk, roll out on a floured board and cut into rounds with a large cookie cutter. Dip each roll in melted butter and fold in half. Place rolls side by side in a buttered baking pan and allow to rise in a warm place for 30 minutes or so. Bake in a preheated 425° oven for about 20 minutes, or until nicely browned.

For Cloverleaf Rolls: After the dough has risen to double in bulk, punch it down and form small balls of dough by rolling between your palms. Dip the balls in melted butter and place 3 in each cup of a buttered muffin tin. Allow to rise in a warm place until doubled in bulk. Preheat the oven to 425° and bake for 15 to 20 minutes, or until nicely browned.

Makes 2 dozen

PRUNE PUDDING

Prune pudding, unlike the Plum Pudding in the following recipe, is a very light dessert, a sweet, airy foam for those who have had enough substantial fare and want to close on a delicate note.

6 egg whites
½ teaspoon cream of tartar
1 cup sugar
¾ cup stewed prunes, puréed or sieved
1 tablespoon vanilla extract
½ cup chopped nuts (optional)

Preheat the oven to 250°. Butter a 9-inch square pan. Beat the egg whites until foamy. Add the cream of tartar and continue beating until soft peaks form. Add the sugar, 1 tablespoon at a time, until all of the sugar is incorporated and the egg whites are stiff but not dry.

Flavor the prunes with the vanilla. Fold into the beaten egg whites along with chopped nuts. Pour into the buttered pan and cover with aluminum foil. Place the pan in a larger pan of hot water. Bake for 30 minutes. Remove the foil and continue baking for another 30 minutes, until crispy on top. Serve warm or chilled with whipped cream.

Serves 6

PLUM PUDDING WITH HARD SAUCE

This is a form of the traditional English steamed plum pudding. It is rich with a variety of fruits, not including plums, and is saturated with spirits. Serve it with the sweet, buttery Hard Sauce that follows.

3 to 4 cups fine dried bread crumbs or pound cake crumbs
½ teaspoon salt
¾ teaspoon ground cinnamon
½ teaspoon ground nutmeg
¼ teaspoon ground cloves
1 cup packed brown sugar
¾ cup milk, scalded
6 eggs, beaten
1 cup ground suet
1½ cups dark raisins
½ cup currants
¼ cup chopped candied orange peel
¼ cup chopped candied lemon peel
¼ cup chopped citron
¼ cup chopped dates
½ cup rum, brandy, cider or bourbon whiskey

In a bowl, combine the crumbs with the salt, spices and brown sugar. Stir in the scalded milk and allow to cool. Mix in the eggs and suet, then add all of the fruits and liquor. Mix well. Place in a buttered pudding mold. Top with a sheet of foil and seal with a lid or another layer of foil.

Stand the mold on a rack in the bottom of a large, tall pan. Pour enough boiling water into the larger pan to reach halfway up the sides of the mold. Steam over low heat for 4 to 5 hours, replenishing the boiling water as necessary throughout the steaming. Serve with Hard Sauce.

Serves 12

HARD SAUCE

1 cup (2 sticks) unsalted butter, at room temperature
1½ cups confectioners' sugar
1 teaspoon vanilla extract
1 tablespoon bourbon whiskey, rum or cognac

In a bowl, cream the butter until fluffy. Gradually add the sugar, vanilla and bourbon. Mix until smooth.

Makes 1½ cups

MINCEMEAT CAKE

Mincemeat usually appears at Thanksgiving and Christmas in the form of mincemeat pies. If you are partial to mincemeat and would like an alternative to the inevitable pie, you might like to try this substantial iced cake as a variation.

2 cups all-purpose flour
1 teaspoon ground mace
1½ teaspoons ground cinnamon
1 teaspoon salt
1 cup buttermilk
1 teaspoon baking soda
1 cup vegetable oil
5 eggs
2 cups sugar
1 teaspoon vanilla extract
1½ cups wet mincemeat
¾ cup chopped pecans

Preheat the oven to 300°. Butter and flour two 8-inch round cake pans. Sift together the flour, mace, cinnamon and salt; set aside. Beat the buttermilk and soda until the mixture is light; set aside. In a bowl, beat together the oil, eggs, sugar and vanilla. Add the sifted ingredients to the egg mixture alternately with the buttermilk mixture. Stir in the mincemeat and pecans.

Divide the batter between the pans. Bake for 45 minutes to 1 hour, until a toothpick inserted in the center comes out clean. Cool on a rack. Unmold. Frost with the icing below.

ICING:

2½ cups packed light brown sugar
1 cup heavy cream
½ cup (1 stick) butter, at room temperature
1 teaspoon vanilla extract

Combine the sugar and cream in a heavy saucepan and cook to the soft ball stage, 234° to 238°, or until it forms a soft ball when dropped in cold water. Turn off the heat, add the butter and vanilla and beat until creamy.

Serves 12

Some Cookies For Tea

Life—even between Christmas and New Year's—cannot be an endless cocktail party if you value your liver, your sanity and your reputation. The round of both casual and formal social events at this time—including mid-afternoon as well as evening entertainments—militates against regarding the bar as the appropriate source of refreshment on all such occasions. Better to serve a tea.

The English have made an art of serving tea and the delicacies that go with it, mostly cakes, cookies and little sandwiches. The custom was once widely popular in this country, too, and seems to be regaining favor in our big cities these days, now that some of our best hotels and restaurants have rediscovered the art of serving tea. In Kentucky, the taking of tea in the late afternoon never disappeared, since it is such a pleasant and sensible way to entertain. My aunts and grandmother regularly entertained the ladies of the Coterie Club at tea, and I suspect they would all have developed severe withdrawal symptoms if their tea parties had suddenly ended. And the custom isn't confined to ladies: When a gentleman develops that hollow feeling toward the end of the day, there's nothing like a cuppa and a plate of fine baked goods to put things right.

Tea service can range from the truly formidable display of china, silver and damask often assembled in Kentucky, to a simple earthenware pot of tea and a plate of assorted cookies.

I like to serve a popular tea blend such as Prince of Wales or the bergamot-flavored Earl Grey; the more assertive teas like Lapsang Suchong or Russian Caravan are too exotic to be pleasant at teatime, although I do like them first thing in the morning. Lapsang Suchong, I find, has a flavor of smoke and iodine like a single malt, pot-stilled Scotch whiskey, while Russian Caravan is very earthy.

At teatime it's a good idea to have a pot of good coffee on hand, preferably a dark roast, because a lot of Americans just aren't tea drinkers. On cold days, or if there are going to be children at tea, hot chocolate is nice. In late December, when the snow is drifting past the windows, more adults than you might expect will opt for a cup of cocoa if it's offered. Here are some cookies and cakes that you might want to serve at tea, although others in this chapter or the rest of the book would be equally appropriate. And the savory sandwiches in the Derby chapter make fine teatime refreshments.

If you're going to serve several plates of cookies it's a good idea to get as much contrast as possible among the varieties you choose. There are three cookies in this section and others scattered about the book. Orange/Coconut Slice Cookies have that chewy, old-fashioned quality belonging to any oatmeal cookie, of which this is a variation. Ginger Sparkles have the flavor of sweetened ginger and a glittering surface achieved by rolling them in sugar before baking. The Date Squares are dense, chewy, sticky fruit and nut bars.

ORANGE/COCONUT SLICE COOKIES

1 cup granulated sugar
1 cup packed brown sugar
1 cup (2 sticks) butter, at room temperature
2 eggs
2 cups all-purpose flour
1 teaspoon baking powder
1 teaspoon baking soda
1½ teaspoons salt
1 teaspoon vanilla extract
2 cups rolled oats
1 cup shredded coconut
½ cup fresh orange juice
¾ cup confectioners' sugar

Preheat the oven to 325°. In a bowl, cream both sugars with the butter. Beat in the eggs. Sift together the flour, baking powder, baking soda and salt. Add to the creamed mixture. Add the vanilla, oats and coconut and mix thoroughly. Roll out into 1-inch balls and place on an ungreased baking sheet. Flatten out with a spatula.

Bake for 12 to 15 minutes, or until browned. Mix together the orange juice and confectioners' sugar. Glaze the cookies while still warm.

Makes 2 dozen

GINGER SPARKLES

¾ **cup shortening**
1½ **cups sugar**
1 egg
¼ **cup molasses**
2 cups all-purpose flour
1 tablespoon ground ginger
2 teaspoons baking soda
1 teaspoon ground cinnamon
¼ **teaspoon salt**

Preheat the oven to 350°. Cream the shortening, gradually adding 1 cup of the sugar until fluffy. Beat in the egg and molasses.

Measure the flour, ginger, baking soda, cinnamon and salt into a sifter and sift over the shortening mixture; blend well. The dough should be stiff enough to handle.

Form teaspoonfuls of dough into marble-size balls by rolling between the palms. Roll each ball in the remaining ½ cup to coat completely. Place 2 inches apart on an ungreased baking sheet.

Bake for 12 to 15 minutes, or until the tops are crackled and lightly browned. Remove with a spatula and cool completely on a wire rack.

Makes 3 dozen

DATE SQUARES

½ **cup (1 stick) butter**
1 cup sugar
2 eggs, lightly beaten
8 ounces pitted dates, finely chopped
1 cup finely chopped pecans
1 cup shredded coconut

Melt the butter in the top of a double boiler over simmering water. Stir in the sugar and eggs. Heat over simmering water, stirring every 5 minutes, for 20 to 30 minutes, or until the mixture is thick and coats the back of a wooden spoon. Pour over the dates, add the nuts and mix well.

Allow to cool to room temperature. Pat the dough into a 9-inch square pan. Cover with the coconut. Store airtight. Slice into bars for serving.

Makes 2 dozen

AUNT MABEL'S ORANGE FRUIT CAKE

My Aunt Mabel Felts converted any number of folks usually in-different to fruitcake by serving them this lovely, orange-flavored cake. It is especially delightful with tea. The cake has traveled as far abroad as Texas with my Aunt Florence, who discovered that it stays moist if wrapped tightly in orange juice-soaked cheesecloth.

CAKE

3½ cups sifted flour
½ teaspoon salt
2 cups diced orange jelly candies or gum drops
1 cup chopped pitted dates
2 cups chopped walnuts or pecans
½ cup shredded coconut
1 cup butter
2 cups sugar
4 eggs
1 teaspoon baking soda
½ cup buttermilk

ORANGE GLAZE:

1 cup orange juice
2 cups confectioners' sugar

Preheat the oven to 300°. Grease and flour a 10-inch tube pan.

Sift together the flour and salt. Combine the orange candies, dates, walnuts and coconut; add ½ cup of the flour mixture. In a large bowl, cream the butter until light. Gradually add the sugar, while beating. Beat well. One at a time, add the eggs, beating thoroughly after each addition. Combine the baking soda and but-termilk. Add alternately with the flour mixture, blending well after each addition. Add the candy mixture and mix well.

Turn into the pan and bake for 1 hour and 45 minutes.

Combine the ingredients for the Orange Glaze and blend thoroughly.

Pour over the hot cake and let cool completely. Refrigerate the cake for 24 hours before removing it from the pan.

Serves 12

New Year's Eve Supper

I am not a big fan of New Year's Eve as it is ordinarily celebrated. It has always seemed to me that everyone feels it a duty to have a good time, tries too hard and almost invariably fails. I'm not enamored of excessive noise or party hats, throw-away horns or paper streamers; and amateur night among the drinkers can get hard to bear. I suspect the frantic gaiety is an effort to drown out the reflections, sometimes happy, sometimes sad, that always accompany the end of one year and the beginning of another. I'd rather deal with my year-end thoughts about life head-on, without trying to blot out what is past. As a wise old woman I knew in Campbellsville put it, "Just leave it lay where Jesus flung it."

Consequently, my idea of a good New Year's Eve is to have a few friends in for dinner and an evening of conversation or cards before the fire. Good food, good drink, laughter and companionship in comfortable and familiar surroundings are as happy and civilized an answer to the question of what to do about New Year's as I know. Here are some suggestions for a relaxed but festive New Year's Eve supper to be served late with champagne. To begin there is Cream of Shrimp Soup followed by Chicken Breasts with Ham Stuffing. I round out the meal by serving wild rice, baked tomatoes, Pocketbook Rolls (page 199) and a salad with Sauce Vinaigrette (page 34). White Chocolate Cake is the dessert and Bourbon Cookies are passed with coffee.

CREAM OF SHRIMP SOUP

This rich soup is faintly pink and brimming with shrimp. The presentation is nicer if you can get quite small shrimp for this soup but if necessary cut larger shrimp into appropriate-size pieces.

¼ cup (½ stick) butter
¼ cup all-purpose flour
1 small onion, grated
3 cups milk
2 teaspoons cayenne pepper
1 teaspoon salt
1 teaspoon freshly ground white pepper
1 teaspoon paprika
½ teaspoon Worcestershire sauce
1 cup heavy cream
2 pounds small raw shrimp, peeled and deveined, if desired

In a heavy saucepan, melt the butter. Add the flour and stir over low heat until well combined. Add the onion and gradually add 1 cup of the milk, stirring constantly until thickened. Add the remaining 2 cups of milk and all of the seasonings.

Before serving, add the cream. Heat, but do not boil. Add the shrimp and cook for 5 minutes, or until piping hot. Do not boil.

Serves 6

CHICKEN BREASTS WITH HAM STUFFING

These ham-stuffed chicken breasts combine a number of compatible flavors including chicken, ham, mushrooms and wine. The preparation produces a sauce to serve on the wild rice that accompanies it, and the dish can be prepared in advance and shoved into the oven to bake when you're dummy at bridge.

6 skinless, boneless chicken breast halves
½ cup corn bread crumbs
½ cup fresh bread crumbs
½ cup ground or minced cooked ham (country ham, if possible)
2 tablespoons chopped fresh parsley
1 tablespoon chopped onion
¼ teaspoon salt
⅛ teaspoon freshly ground pepper
¼ cup melted butter
½ cup chicken broth
1 cup white sauce
¼ cup chopped mushrooms
½ cup dry vermouth
½ teaspoon paprika
2 teaspoons cornstarch

Place each chicken breast half between two sheets of waxed paper and pound lightly. In a bowl, combine both kinds of bread crumbs, the ham, parsley, onion, salt and pepper. Toss lightly with the melted butter and broth until moistened.

Divide the stuffing among the pounded chicken breasts. Fold the chicken around the stuffing, tucking in the ends. Secure with toothpicks, if necessary. Place the chicken breasts, folded side down, in a buttered oblong baking dish. Mix the white sauce, mushrooms and vermouth; pour over the chicken. Sprinkle with the paprika. Cover and refrigerate until serving time.

Preheat the oven to 350°. Bake the chicken for 1 hour, or until tender and browned. Place the chicken on a heated platter. Mix the cornstarch into ¼ cup water and stir into the sauce. Cook, stirring, until thick. Serve the sauce on the side, with wild rice.

Serves 6

WHITE CHOCOLATE CAKE

I received the recipe for this rich, elegant pound cake, as well as several other recipes in this book, from Mildred Eblen Elliott, an authority on Kentucky cooking and a wonderful hostess. She and her friend, Elizabeth Kremer, were instrumental in starting the wonderful Shaker restaurant, Trustee's House, at the Shakertown community of Pleasant Hill.

½ **pound white chocolate, coarsely chopped**
1 **cup (2 sticks) butter, at room temperature**
2 **cups sugar**
4 **eggs**
2½ **cups cake flour**
1 **teaspoon baking powder**
¼ **teaspoon salt**
1 **cup buttermilk**
1 **cup shredded coconut**
1 **teaspoon vanilla extract**
1 **cup chopped pecans**

Preheat the oven to 350°. Butter and flour a 10-inch tube pan. Melt the white chocolate over simmering water in a double boiler. Allow to cool slightly. In a bowl, cream the butter and sugar until smooth. Add the chocolate and then, one at a time, add the eggs, beating well after each addition.

Sift together the flour, baking powder and salt. Add to the batter alternately with the buttermilk. Fold in the coconut, vanilla and pecans. Pour the batter into the prepared pan. Bake for about 1 hour and 15 minutes until a toothpick inserted in the center comes out clean. Cool in the pan for 5-10 minutes. Run a knife around the edge of the pan to loosen the cake. Invert onto a rack to cool completely and then frost.

FROSTING:

2 cups sugar
1 cup (2 sticks) butter
¾ cup condensed milk
1 teaspoon vanilla extract
¼ teaspoon salt

In a heavy saucepan, combine all of the ingredients and cook, stirring, until the frosting reaches the soft ball stage, 234° to 238°, or forms a soft ball when dropped into cold water. Remove from the heat and beat until cooled and very smooth.

Serves 10 to 15

BOURBON COOKIES

These pale, seductive cookies have a hint of one of Kentucky's favorite flavors—bourbon whiskey. The alcohol bakes out but the essence remains. The cookies themselves are crisp and wonderful with tea, but they are especially appropriate for festive occasions like New Year's Eve Supper or on a Derby Day buffet.

1 cup (2 sticks) butter, at room temperature
1 teaspoon vanilla extract
1⅓ cups sugar
2 eggs
2⅓ cups sifted all-purpose flour
¼ teaspoon cream of tartar
¼ teaspoon salt
⅓ cup sour cream
⅓ cup bourbon whiskey

Preheat the oven to 375°. Butter a baking sheet. In a bowl, cream together the butter, vanilla and sugar until very smooth. Add the eggs, 1 at a time, beating well after each addition. Sift together the flour, cream of tartar and salt. Stir into the mixture alternately with the sour cream and bourbon. Drop the dough by teaspoonfuls onto the cookie sheet. Bake for 10 minutes, until lightly browned. Cool on a rack.

Makes 6 dozen

New Year's Day

Well, I hope you will take to heart my advice about New Year's Eve and that therefore you'll feel your best on New Year's Day. It's a good day for greeting the New Year and for saying farewell to another holiday season which often, by this time, is beginning to seem longer than Charles de Gaulle's overcoat. Here are some dishes for a triumphant holiday menu that will do you proud, and speed your friends and relations toward starting the year right, perhaps by starting a post-holiday diet. Do keep in mind that the Black-Eyed Peas are essential if you expect to have a happy and prosperous year.

OYSTER STEW

Kentucky does not have coasts teeming with oyster beds, yet for many years oysters have been a beloved part of holiday fare at home. I believe they were originally shipped up the river from New Orleans, packed in barrels of ice embedded in sawdust on fast paddle wheelers. Later, transportation became easier and oysters became less of a rarity but no less esteemed. A plain oyster on the half shell with just a squeeze of lemon and a grind of pepper can hardly be improved upon, so if you wish to cook oysters, my advice is: the simpler the recipe the better. This recipe is true to that advice.

¼ **cup (½ stick) butter**
½ **teaspoon or more grated onion or leek**
1 to 1½ pints shucked oysters, with their liquor

1 cup milk
1 cup heavy cream
½ teaspoon salt
⅛ teaspoon freshly ground white pepper or paprika
2 tablespoons chopped fresh parsley
¼ cup dry white wine

Combine the butter and onion in the top of a double boiler over hot water and sauté lightly. Add the oysters with their liquor, the milk, cream, salt and pepper. Place over boiling water and cook until piping hot. Add the chopped parsley. Just before serving, add the wine and cook for 30 seconds.

Serves 4

ROAST SUCKLING PIG WITH SAUSAGE STUFFING

There is always less to roast suckling pig than meets the eye. A whole roast pig, an apple in its mouth and cranberries in its eyes, always looks immense when carried in on its platter, as though it would serve Henry VIII, all his wives, twelve lords-a-leaping, the Rockettes and the Brigade of Guards. However, the amount of meat you can carve off it always proves less than you expected. Consequently I like to use a sausage stuffing, which assures that everyone gets plenty of meat and is a delicious addition to the meal in its own right. Incidentally, this stuffing also goes well with turkey or with a breast of veal.

SAUSAGE STUFFING:

1 pound bulk country sausage
3 cups cooked white rice or dried bread crumbs
2 tablespoons chopped celery leaves
2 tablespoons chopped chives
1 tablespoon chopped fresh parsley
1 tablespoon poultry seasoning
1 teaspoon salt
1 teaspoon freshly ground pepper

PIG:

14- to 16-pound suckling pig
½ cup (1 stick) butter, softened
Salt and freshly ground pepper
1 cup all-purpose flour

1 small red apple
2 cranberries

Prepare the sausage stuffing: Cook the sausage and drain off the fat, reserving 2 tablespoonfuls. In a large bowl, combine all of the remaining stuffing ingredients. Add 2 tablespoons of the reserved fat and mix thoroughly with your hands.

Preheat the oven to 300°. Use a butcher-prepared pig, cleaned and washed. Force the mouth open and insert a piece of wood to keep it open while roasting. Stuff the cavity with the sausage dressing and sew up the opening. Place on a rack in an open roasting pan with the forefeet extended. Fold the hind legs under and tie or skewer them in place. Rub the pig with the butter. Sprinkle with salt and pepper and dust with the flour. Add 3 cups of water to the roasting pan to create steam.

Fold foil around the ears and tail to protect them from burning. Roast for 2½ hours, basting every 15 minutes with the hot water and drippings. Remove the foil and roast for 30 minutes to 1 hour, until a meat thermometer reaches 180°. Remove the wood; place the apple in the mouth and cranberries in the eyes. Serve.

Serves 12 to 15

BRUSSELS SPROUTS AND CHESTNUTS

This recipe was almost assigned to the Christmas dinner menu because it goes so well with roast beef. The brussels sprouts and the chestnuts complement one another wonderfully both in texture and in flavor.

2 cups brussels sprouts
1½ cups canned or jarred chestnuts
½ cup (1 stick) butter
1 teaspoon ground mace
½ teaspoon salt
2 tablespoons heavy cream

Put the brussels sprouts in a saucepan with just enough water to cover. Bring to a boil, cover and cook over moderate heat for 20 to 25 minutes, until just tender. Drain and return to the pan.

In a separate pan, cook the chestnuts in boiling water for 15 minutes. Drain and add to the sprouts along with the butter, mace, salt and cream. Simmer for 5 minutes. Serve hot.

Serves 4 to 6

BLACK-EYED PEAS

Black-eyed peas bring luck in the New Year as every Southerner knows. Some insist that the black-eyed peas must be made into Hoppin' John, in which the peas are combined with rice. I suppose Hoppin' John provides complete protein, being a classic legume/rice combination, but I'm here to tell you that your luck won't be any worse if you leave out the rice. Most people find this a better dish.

**2 cups dried black-eyed peas, washed and soaked for at least
    6 hours
1½ pounds salt pork, cut into strips
1 large onion, pierced with 6 cloves
1 carrot, halved
1 bay leaf
1 teaspoon freshly ground coarse black pepper
¼ cup sour cream
¼ cup minced onion**

In a saucepan, cover the peas with 6 cups of water and bring to a boil. Reduce the heat to low and add the salt pork, whole onion, carrot, bay leaf and pepper. Simmer, partially covered, for 30 to 45 minutes, until tender. Remove the onion. Serve, garnished with the sour cream and minced onion.

Serves 8

CHARLOTTE RUSSE WITH RASPBERRY SAUCE

I don't know who Charlotte was or what she did to get so many desserts and a dessert pan named after her. Maybe she was nice to chefs or maybe she just had a monumental sweet tooth. Anyhow, here she is in her Russian mode. I don't see anything particularly

Russian about this combination, either, come to think of it, but perhaps some French chef thought all these pale ingredients suggested winter on the Steppes. It gets a splash of color from the raspberry sauce that accompanies it.

This dessert employs the classic charlotte formula of a molded ladyfinger-lined flavored pudding. If you want a second dessert, try the Applesauce/Pineapple Christmas Cake that follows—I know it's after Christmas, but no one will mind if you tell your guests it's Applesauce/Pineapple New Year's Cake.

1½ envelopes unflavored gelatin
2 cups milk
4 egg yolks
1½ cups sugar
¼ cup sweet sherry, or 2 tablespoons almond extract
1½ teaspoons unsalted butter
36 fresh ladyfingers (about ½ pound)
4 cups heavy cream, whipped
4 egg whites, stiffly beaten

Soak the gelatin in ½ cup of the milk. Scald the remaining 1½ cups milk in the top of a double boiler over simmering water. In a bowl, beat the egg yolks and sugar. Gradually add the scalded milk, stirring constantly to prevent the yolks from scrambling. When all of the milk is incorporated, return the mixture to the double boiler and cook, stirring constantly, until it forms a soft custard. Stir in the sherry and gelatin. Allow to cool to room temperature.

Coat a 9-inch springform pan with the butter. Line the sides of the mold with the ladyfingers, reserving enough to cover the top. Gently fold the whipped cream and beaten egg whites into the cooled custard. Pour into the mold and cover the top with the reserved ladyfingers. Chill for at least 3 hours. Unmold and serve with raspberry sauce.

Serves 12

RASPBERRY SAUCE

2 cups sieved red raspberries (pulp and juice)
½ cup red currant jelly
½ cup sugar
2 tablespoons cold water

In a nonreactive saucepan, combine the raspberries, jelly and sugar; bring to a boil. Add the cold water, stirring constantly. Continue to cook until thick and clear. Let cool.

Makes about 2½ cups

APPLESAUCE/PINEAPPLE CHRISTMAS CAKE

This is a form of fruitcake, moistened with applesauce and, if you wish, with bourbon or other spirits. Decorated with fruit and coated with a clear glaze, it looks very festive. Like all fruitcakes it is a substantial, almost heavy dessert and provides a real contrast with the preceding light, creamy molded dessert. The cake keeps well and may be with you well into the New Year.

1 cup (2 sticks) butter
2 cups sugar
3 eggs
½ cup applesauce
3 cups all-purpose flour
1 teaspoon baking soda
1½ teaspoons freshly grated nutmeg
1 teaspoon ground cinnamon
1 teaspoon ground cloves
2 cups drained crushed pineapple
2 tablespoons light corn syrup
1 cup dark raisins
4 cups golden raisins
1 pound mixed candied fruit, chopped

Preheat the oven to 300°. Butter and flour a 9-inch tube pan. In a bowl, cream together the butter and sugar. Beat in the eggs and applesauce. Sift the flour with the baking soda, nutmeg, cinnamon and cloves. Add to the batter alternately with the crushed pineapple. Stir in the corn syrup. Fold in the raisins and candied fruit. Turn into the prepared pan. Bake for 1½ hours, until a toothpick inserted in the center comes out clean. Prepare the glaze.

GLAZE:

½ **cup confectioners' sugar**
½ **cup light corn syrup**
½ **teaspoon cornstarch**
½ **cup pineapple slices**
¼ **cup candied cherries**
¼ **cup bourbon whiskey, wine or rum (optional)**

In a saucepan, combine the sugar, corn syrup and cornstarch. Cook over moderate heat for 5 minutes. Brush on the warm cake. Decorate with the pineapple and cherries.

To age the cake, which improves it by marrying the flavors, place in a tin with a close-fitting lid. Sprinkle a piece of cheesecloth with the bourbon and cover the cake with it. Close and store in a cool place.

Serves 20

LEMON SQUARES

Very simple but very satisfying, these squares are both crisp and chewy. They have an intense lemon flavor.

2¼ **cups all-purpose flour**
½ **cup confectioners' sugar**
1 **cup (2 sticks) unsalted butter**
¾ **cup fresh lemon juice**
2 **cups granulated sugar**
1 **teaspoon baking powder**
4 **eggs, lightly beaten**
¼ **cup confectioners' sugar, for dusting**

Preheat the oven to 350°. In a bowl, combine 2 cups of the flour and the confectioners' sugar. Cut in the butter with a pastry blender or two knives until the dough forms into pea-size clumps. Pat the dough into a 9 x 11-inch pan. Bake for 30 minutes; leave the oven on.

In a bowl, whisk together the remaining ¼ cup flour with the lemon juice, sugar, baking powder and eggs. Pour over the warm crust. Bake for 45 minutes longer. Allow to cool and dust with the confectioners' sugar. Cut into squares to serve.

Makes 1 dozen 3-inch squares

Appendix

ADDRESSES OF KENTUCKY INNS

Below are the addresses of the inns that have contributed recipes to this book.

THE BEAUMONT INN
638 Beaumont Drive
Harrodsburg, Kentucky 40330
(606) 734-3381

BOONE TAVERN OF BEREA COLLEGE
C.P.O. 2345, Main and Prospect
Berea, Kentucky 40404
(606) 986-9359

THE BROWN
Fourth and Broadway
Louisville, Kentucky 40202
(502) 583-1234

THE MANSION AT GRIFFIN GATE
1720 Newton Pike
Lexington, Kentucky 40511
(606) 231-5152

MARIAH'S 1818 RESTAURANT
801 State Street
Bowling Green, Kentucky 42101
(502) 842-6878

THE OLD STONE INN
Simpsonville, Kentucky 40347
(502) 722-8882

THE OLD TALBOTT TAVERN
107 West Stephen Foster
Bardstown, Kentucky 40004
(502) 348-3494

SCIENCE HILL INN
525 Washington Street
Shelbyville, Kentucky 40065
(502) 633-2825

THE SEELBACH HOTEL
500 Fourth Avenue
Louisville, Kentucky 40202
(502) 585-3200

THE SHAKER VILLAGE OF PLEASANT HILL
Route #4
Harrodsburg, Kentucky 40330
(606) 734-5411

KENTUCKY SPECIALTIES: A Mail Order Source List

BALLANCE COUNTRY HAMS
Route 1 Box 15
Oakland, Kentucky 42159
(502) 563-3956

D. L. PENN'S HAMS
Route 6
Campbellsville, Kentucky 42718
(502) 465-5065

ELMWOOD INN KENTUCKY SAUCE
Elmwood Inn
205 4th Street
Perrysville, Kentucky 40468
(606) 332-2271

GOLDEN KENTUCKY PURE CANE
   SORGHUM
Distributed by:
Rockcastle River Community
   Land Trust
Livingston, Kentucky 40445

KENTUCKY DERBY DAY PARTY KIT
Party Kits Unlimited
141 N. Sherrin Avenue
Louisville, Kentucky 40207
(502) 896-0400

MYRTIE FRAZIER'S BEATEN BISCUITS
Route 2 Box 886
Columbia, Kentucky 42728
(502) 384-4127

REBEKAH'S CORN RELISH
Rebekah's-Sun Gold
Cecilia, Kentucky 42724

REBEKAH'S WHITE HOMINY GRITS
THE FAMOUS OLD HOUSE SALAD
   DRESSING
Distributed by:
Ky's Heritage Products
217 Industry Parkway
Nicholasville, Kentucky 40356
(502) 885-5475

Index

apple(s):
  Annie's candied, 105–106
  butternut squash soup
    with, 118–119
  fried, 77–78
  pie, Granny's blue ribbon,
    133-134
  sweet potatoes with, 131
applesauce:
  muffins, 162-163
  pineapple Christmas
    cake, 216–217
apricot sherbet, 40
asparagus:
  with raspberry
    hollandaise, 160–161
  vinaigrette, 33
aspic:
  chicken, 47–48
  cucumber, 178
  seafood, 47
  vegetable, 48

barbecue(d):
  ribs, 72–73
  sauce, 72
beef, standing rib roast of,
    194–195
beverages:
  mint juleps, 21
  sassafras tea, 68–69
biscuit(s):
  buttermilk, 84–85

cornmeal, 56
cream of tartar, 57
James's old Southern
  beaten, 30–31
pudding with bourbon
  sauce, 148–149
yeast buttermilk, 98–99
black bean soup, 69–70
blackberry jam, 99
black-eyed peas, 214
bourbon:
  butter, Kentucky, 100
  cookies, 210–211
  hickory nut whiskey
    cake, 37–38
  Kentucky colonels,
    62–63
  Kentucky sauce, 185
  mint juleps, 21
  pecan cake, 135–136
  pound cake, 110–111
  sauce, biscuit pudding
    with, 148–149
bread:
  cracklin', 83–84
  cranberry, 158
  Kentucky Sally Lunn,
    31–32
  Ma Kate Eblen's
    cinnamon rolls,
    198–200
  popovers, 197
  shortenin', 83

  spoon, 82
  see also corn bread
brownies, 170
brussels sprouts and
  chestnuts, 213–214
burgoo, Taylor county,
  23–25
butter:
  Kentucky bourbon, 100
  pie crust, 60
  and sorghum spread, 85
buttermilk:
  biscuits, 84–85
  cake, 61–62
  yeast biscuits, 98–99

cabbage:
  fit-for-a-king, 81–82
  stuffed, 50–51
cakes:
  applesauce/pineapple
    Christmas, 216–217
  Aunt Mabel's orange fruit,
    206
  bourbon pound, 110–111
  burnt sugar, 106–107
  buttermilk, 61–62
  gingerbread muffins,
    132–133
  hickory nut whiskey,
    37–38
  jam, with caramel icing,
    159

Kentucky funeral, 63
mincemeat, 202
molasses stack, 85–86
pecan bourbon, 135–136
prune, 192–193
scripture, 91
sour cream coffee, 101
sponge, 109
tipsy, 110
white chocolate, 209–210
candy:
  creamy pralines, 138–139
  divinity, 111
  Kentucky colonels, 62–63
  monkey heels (popcorn
    balls), 131–132
caramel:
  boiled custard, 191
  icing, jam cake with, 159
casseroles:
  grits soufflé, 32–33
  scalloped zucchini, 155
  Sicilian potato, 161
  tomato okra, 165
catfish, Green River, with
    hush puppies, 70–72
cheese:
  Benedictine sandwich
    spread, 22
  delights, 102
  the Hot Brown, 151–152
  pimiento sandwiches, 22
cheesecake, Mariah's 1818,
  163
chestnuts and brussels
    sprouts, 213–214
chicken:
  aspic, 47–48
  breasts with ham stuffing,
    208–209
  chow mein, Brown Hotel,
    152–153
  creamed, 26
  Fannie Bell's fried, 179
  flakes in a bird's nest,
    168–169
  and ham pie, 53
chocolate:
  brownies, 170
  pie, racing silks, 38–39

sauce, 185
white, cake, 209–210
cinnamon rolls, Ma Kate
    Eblen's, 198–200
coconut/orange slice
    cookies, 204
cookies and squares:
  boiled, 88
  bourbon, 210–211
  brownies, 170
  date squares, 205
  ginger sparkles, 205
  lemon squares, 217
  Mildred Emerson's
    Christmas, 192
  orange/coconut slice, 204
corn:
  fried, in cream, 74–75
  fritters, 158
  pudding, 145
corn bread:
  and sausage pie, 48–49
  stuffing, 123–124
cornmeal:
  biscuits, 56
  fried mush, 75–76
  griddle cakes, 74
  spoon bread, 82
crabmeat thermidor,
  189–190
crab salad, 177–178
cranberry:
  bread, 158
  mold (Christmas star), 198
cucumber:
  aspic, 178
  pickles, 129

desserts:
  apricot sherbet, 40
  boiled custard, 191
  caramel boiled custard,
    191
  Charlotte Russe with
    raspberry sauce,
    214–216
  Huguenot torte, 146
  Kentucky sauce, 185

Mariah's 1818 cheesecake,
  163
peach cobbler, 186
pears in red wine, 39
pecan tarts, 105
popovers, 197
rhubarb sauce, 59
strawberry fluff, 40–41
strawberry shortcake,
  179–180
see also cakes;
  cookies and squares; ice
  cream;
  pies, dessert;
  puddings
doves, country, 50
duck, autumn, 148

eggplant, stuffed, 156
eggs, curried, in shrimp
  sauce, 97–98

ginger:
  pears, preserved, 77
  sparkles, 205
gingerbread muffins,
  132–133
gravy:
  giblet, 124
  redeye, fried country
    ham with, 97
greens:
  collard, 79–80
  dandelion, 79
  kale, 79–80
  mustard, 79–80
  turnip, 79
grits soufflé casserole,
  32–33

ham:
  and chicken pie, 53
  country, how to
    prepare, 29–30
  country, salad spread,
    103
  fried country, with
    redeye gravy, 96–97

mousse, 176–177
stuffing, chicken
    breasts with, 208–209
hickory nut whiskey cake,
    37–38
horseradish sauce or
    mold, 195–196
hush puppies, Green River
    catfish with, 70–72

ice cream, homemade:
    peach, 183
    peppermint, 183
    vanilla, 181–182
ice cream, sauces for:
    berry, 184
    chocolate, 185
    Kentucky, 185
    pecan, 184
    rum, 184

jam:
    blackberry, 99
    cake with caramel
        icing, 159

lard pie crust, 60–61
lemon:
    pie, Shaker, 136–137
    sauce, 133
    squares, 217
lentil soup, 188
lettuce, wilted, 55

mint:
    juleps, 21
    sauce, fresh, mutton
        loaf with, 104–105
molasses stack cake,
    85–86
monkey heels (popcorn
    balls), 131–132
muffins:
    applesauce, 162–163
    gingerbread, 132–133
mutton loaf with fresh
    mint sauce, 104–105

okra tomato casserole,
    165
onions, creamed, 196–197
orange:
    chess pie, old
        Kentucky, 90
    coconut slice cookies,
        204
    fruit cake, Aunt
        Mabel's, 206
oyster(s):
    scalloped, 188–189
    stew, 211–212

peach:
    cobbler, 186
    ice cream, 183
pears:
    preserved ginger, 77
    in red wine, 39
peas:
    black-eyed, 214
    garden, bisque of,
        165–166
pecan:
    bourbon cake, 135–136
    creamy pralines,
        138–139
    sauce, 184
    tarts, 105
pepper, green:
    jelly, 128
    puddin', 55–56
    and red pepper relish,
        128–129
peppermint ice cream, 183
pickles:
    cucumber, 129
    watermelon rind,
        129–130
pies, dessert:
    brown sugar, 90
    butterscotch, 108
    chess, 137–138
    Granny's blue ribbon
        apple, 133–134
    green tomato, 87–88

Jefferson Davis, 169
Lonzetta's pumpkin,
    134–135
old Kentucky orange
    chess, 90
Pegasus, 171
racing silks chocolate,
    38–39
rhubarb, 58–59
Shaker lemon, 136–137
stack, 166–167
sweet potato, 86–87
vinegar, 89
pies, savory:
    ham and chicken, 53
    sausage and corn bread,
        48–49
    veal and sweetbreads,
        190–191
pie crust:
    butter, 60
    lard, 60–61
pig, roast suckling, with
    sausage stuffing,
    212–213
pimiento cheese
    sandwiches, 22
pineapple/applesauce
    Christmas cake,
    216–217
plum pudding with hard
    sauce, 201
popcorn balls, 131–132
popovers, 197
pork:
    Campbellsville-style,
        51–53
    sausage, making and
        cooking, 121
    tenderloin with mustard
        sauce, 147
potato(es):
    casserole, Sicilian,
        161
    Gleating's, 80
    salad, French, 102–103
pralines, creamy, 138–139
prune:
    cake, 192–193
    pudding, 200

puddings:
  biscuit, with bourbon
      sauce, 148–149
  corn, 145
  green pepper, 55–56
  Kentucky tombstone, 139
  plum, with hard sauce,
      201
  prune, 200
  summer, Lafayette,
      180–181
pumpkin pie, Lonzetta's,
    134–135
punch, tea, 176

raspberry:
  hollandaise, asparagus
      with, 160–161
  sauce, Charlotte Russe
      with, 214–216
redeye gravy, fried
    country ham, 96–97
rhubarb:
  pie, 58
  sauce, 59
ribs, barbecued, 72–73

salads:
  country ham, spread,
      103
  crab, 177–178
  Niçoise, Aunt Lizzie's,
      53–54
  potato, French, 102–103
  wilted lettuce, 55
salmon, grilled, with
    herbs, 154
sandwich(es):
  the Hot Brown, 151–152
  pimiento cheese, 22
  spread, Benedictine, 22
sassafras tea, 68–69
sauces:
  barbecue, 72
  berry, 184
  chocolate, 185
  custard, 191
  hard, 201

hollandaise, 160
horseradish, 195–196
Kentucky, 185
lemon, 133
pecan, 184
raspberry, 161
rhubarb, 59
rum, 184
sherry custard, 41
sausage:
  balls, 23
  and corn bread pie,
      48–49
  pork, making and
      cooking, 121
  stuffing, roast
      suckling pig with,
      212–213
scalloped:
  oysters, 188–189
  zucchini, 155
seafood aspic, 47
shrimp:
  sauce, curried eggs in,
      97–98
  soup, cream of, 207–208
sorghum and butter
    spread, 85
soufflé casserole, grits,
    32–33
soups:
  acorn squash, 118
  bisque of garden peas,
      165–166
  black bean, 69–70
  butternut squash, with
      apples, 118–119
  cream of shrimp,
      207–208
  lentil, 188
spreads:
  Benedictine sandwich,
      22
  country ham salad, 103
  pimiento cheese
      sandwiches, 22
  sorghum and butter, 85
squash:
  acorn, soup, 118

butternut, soup with
    apples, 118–119
strawberry:
  shortcake, 179–180
  fluff, 40–41
stuffing:
  corn bread, 123–124
  ham, chicken breasts
      with, 208–209
  sausage, roast suckling
      pig with, 212–213
sweet potato(es):
  with apples, 131
  pie, 86–87

tea:
  punch, 176
  sassafras, 68–69
tomato(es):
  fried, 76
  green, pie, 87–88
  okra cassserole, 165
turkey:
  the Hot Brown, 151–152
  roast, 122–123

vanilla ice cream,
    181–182
veal:
  scallopini, Seelbach
      Hotel, 153
  and sweetbreads pie,
      190–191
vegetable aspic, 48
venison roast, 125
vinaigrette:
  asparagus, 33
  sauce, 34
vinegar pie, 89

waffles, bluegrass, 25
watermelon rind pickles
    129–130
whiskey, *see* bourbon
wine, red, pears in, 39

zucchini, scalloped, 155